**White Militancy
in Boston**

White Militancy in Boston

A Reconsideration of Marx and Weber

Daniel J. Friedman

Lexington Books
D.C. Heath and Company
Lexington, Massachusetts
Toronto   London

Library of Congress Cataloging in Publication Data

Friedman, Daniel J.
    White militancy in Boston: a reconsideration of
Marx and Weber.

    Bibliography: p.
    I. Boston- Race question. I. Title.
F73.52.F74   301.45'1'0420974461   72-12955
ISBN 0-669-85282-1

Published simultaneously in Canada.

Printed in the United States of America.

International Standard Book Number: 0-669-85282-1

Library of Congress Catalog Card Number:

Too often, I feel events scurrying off on their own straight paths while I am left with an imaginary construct, an elaborate framework. . . .[1]

Stephen Tracy

I find myself surrounded by miseries I can no longer cope with. So I want to try a vaster, more encompassing remedy. I would have preferred a collective analysis, but since that is not possible, let us try Marxism.[2]

Anaïs Nin

Contents

List of Figures

ix

List of Tables

Foreword

Social theory as it developed in the late 1950's and early 1960's both described and approved what it saw as the growing consensus, the decline of conflicts and tensions, within western societies. The thesis of the "end of ideology" correct as it was in certain aspects of its analysis, helped to turn attention away from the potential sources of social strain that persisted, or were even growing, in countries like the United States. As a result, the upheavals of the 1960's cannot be adequately dealt with by the social theory we inherited.

More recently, social scientists of various normative persuasions have sought to understand the agitations of the last decade. We now have a considerable body of work detailing various aspects of student radicalism, black and white discontent, and political alienation. Daniel Friedman's book provides us with an opportunity to assess the discussions of discontent in American society, as well as to reflect more generally on the uses of social theory.

Friedman is interested in the rather circumscribed phenomenon of white militancy in reaction to black rioting. His information comes from a survey in Boston, not one of the most riot-torn cities. Yet in attempting to comprehend white attitudes, Friedman ranges into the formidable theoretical worlds of Marx and Weber in an effort to establish a sensible framework for social analysis. His book, then, becomes as much a commentary on one attempt to apply Marxian and Weberian notions to a contemporary situation of conflict, as it is a study of that conflict itself.

Friedman's reading of Marx is distinctly off-beat and requires a reassessment of much that is common in social science treatments of Marx. In particular, Friedman finds Marx's ideas about class structure and class militancy far more flexible than have most others. He is able to derive from Marx a set of hypotheses that serve as the theoretical setting for his study. The subsequent results show both some of the limitations and strengths of this mode of understanding. Friedman, like some others, finds Marx's framework inadequate unless supplemented by Weber's insights — specifically that the hierarchies of class, status and power, do not coincide in modern societies, unlike Marx's expectations.

His use of Marx and Weber provides Friedman with a way of judging other analyses of black and white militancy. He offers a valuable series of evaluations of attitudinal studies of the riots, noting particularly their absence of theoretical underpinnings. The main message of the Friedman book to social scientists is that detailed studies of important contemporary events are best carried on *within* some consciously arrived at theoretical framework, one that we can hammer out and rework as research proceeds.

xiii

The results of Friedman's survey among Boston whites also help shed light on the nature of current tensions in American society. He explores the relative importance of economic, political and status dissatisfactions and their relationships to feelings of militancy toward blacks and toward government. The findings are sometimes revealing and Friedman's interpretations within a semi-Marxist framework are provocative. Perhaps most important, he emphasizes the mediating role of dissatisfactions in shaping people's attitudes toward action, rather than their perception of their low status alone.

Friedman is critical of the ideal of value-free research. Keeping to his rejection of that notion, the book argues for a re-interpretation of white discontent — one that looks for the sources of white as well as black dissatisfactions in the economic, status and political inequalities in contemporary America. I have some reservations about this conclusion, particularly since racism and its offshoots may have psychological origins not related to inequality alone. Still, Friedman's approach helps to remedy the one-sidedness of research that overlooks the possible relationships among whites of inequalities and dissatisfaction related to race. America may be a racist society, but the exact meaning, origin, and significance of racial attitudes is not simple to unravel. Friedman's approach pushes us toward a renewed encounter with the imprints of inequality.

Lewis Lipsitz

Preface

. . . the educator himself needs educating. [1]

Karl Marx

1964-1972: A Changing Perspective on American Violence

American whites were surprised when, in 1964, urban blacks throughout the United States rioted. Even though the rioting was widespread and intense, it was first regarded as a temporary phenomenon. Journalists and politicians initially reacted as if riots were novel occurrences in American history. It was not until later that many commentators realized that the 1960's riots were neither unique nor, relative to past American riots, particularly bloody.

There was, however, one distinguishing feature of the 1960's riots. Previous urban race riots, such as the 1919 Chicago riot and the 1943 Detroit riot, involved clashes between groups of whites and groups of blacks.[2] Mass violence in most earlier riots emanated from both racial groups.[3] In the 1960's, however, the riots were centered in black neighborhoods. The white community was directly involved only when its individual members were in the riot area. Policemen, firemen, and store owners became surrogates for the entire white community and black violence was directed at them.[4] Despite the differences in form from earlier mass racial violence, the 1960's riots can be interpreted not only as arising from interracial tensions, but also as interracial clashes.

Within four years after the rioting began it had, for the most part, ended. Those four years of massive and widespread civil violence led political scientists and sociologists to focus their attention upon the newly recognized problem of American violence. Empirical studies were conducted of black communities in which rioting occurred and attempts were made to discover what caused the riots.

Academic speculations were ventured about the possible consequences of the violence. But this speculation was largely restricted to the consequences of the violence for the black community. Relatively little academic attention was focused on the effects of the riots on the attitudes and actions of urban whites.

Journalists and politicians were quicker than academicians to realize that black violence was a problem which had deep repercussions in white urban areas. Throughout the mid-1960's, journalists wrote of the "white backlash." Such dissimilar politicians as George Wallace — a rural, Anglo-Saxon, southerner — and Louise Day Hicks — an urban, Irish, northerner — supposedly both led and embodied this burgeoning white backlash. Despite the relatively poor showings

xv

of both Hicks and Wallace in the 1967 and 1968 elections, white backlash talk increased. Now, however, the discussion took on a new dimension: under the aegis of Richard Nixon, journalists concerned themselves with the "silent majority." Filling in the unspoken word, *Time, Newsweek,* and *Harper's* all published articles on the silent *white* majority.[5] These articles were largely based on the assumption that "middle America" was reacting to both black mass violence and to the governmental rewards which this violence supposedly evoked.[6]

A 1969 Gallup poll commissioned by *Newsweek* asked "the troubled American" if "Negroes today have a better chance or worse chance than other people like yourself," "what should be done about Negro demands for better education," and "would you agree or disagree that black militants have been treated too leniently." By the nature of the questions asked, *Newsweek* editors largely assumed that white, middle class dissatisfactions derived from anger over black demands, black actions, and the government's policies which were aimed at the black population. The existence of white backlash was less tested than assumed.

Academic research on white backlash often shared similar biases. Although attitudinal research on this problem was surprisingly rare, two fine studies were completed. The first of these was conducted by social scientists at the University of California, Los Angeles, in the five months following the Watts riot. "The White Reaction Study," by Richard T. Morris and Vincent Jeffries, examines white attitudes toward the riot, and briefly deals with the possibility of white violence in two key questions:

Did you approve of white people buying guns to protect themselves during the (riot)?
Did you, at any time, consider using firearms to protect yourself or your family?

The second study, "Racial Attitudes in Fifteen American Cities," was completed in 1968 by the Survey Research Center for the National Advisory Commission on Civil Disorders. Included in the study was a question which sought to determine the attitudinal support and potential for white counter-rioting:

Some people say that if Negroes riot in (Central City) next summer, maybe whites should do some rioting against them. Others say such matters should be left entirely to the authorities to handle. What do you think?

Both studies reveal support for whites taking violent actions against blacks. In "The White Reaction Study," Morris and Jeffries find that 37% of Los Angeles area white men considered using firearms to protect themselves and their families against black rioters.[7] Campbell and Schuman, the authors of "Racial Attitudes in Fifteen American Cities," discover that 11% of black males interviewed say that they would join in a riot, and 8% of white males interviewed support white counter-rioting against blacks.[8] Despite the alarming nature of these findings, they received little attention in the media or in the academic community.

The difficulties inherent in much of the academic research and journalistic speculation on white support for group violence are not methodological, but conceptual. Many of us too readily accepted the Kerner Commission's famous 1968 pronouncement: "White racism is essentially responsible for the explosive mixture which has been accumulating in our cities since the end of World War II."[9] White racism was undoubtedly the major direct and indirect cause of the violence in black communities. However, it takes peculiarly perverse logic to interpret the Kerner Commission statement to mean that: "White racism is essentially responsible for white violence and white support for violence." Just as various kinds of economic, social, and political dissatisfactions — which resulted from white racism — led to black riots, similar dissatisfactions — which do not result from white racism — may cause white violence. Journalists and academicians frequently failed to consider the possibility that many whites, like many blacks, feel basically dissatisfied with American society and politics.[10]

Two events forced commentators to reexamine their assumptions about the causes of white support for militant protest activities. In early October of 1969, white building trades workers in Chicago held a large protest demonstration. The demonstration was directed against an imminent "hometown" agreement between unions, local government, and the federal government, which would have increased the number of blacks trained for construction industry jobs and admitted to the union. The construction workers' fears were not that blacks would get jobs but that whites would lose jobs. As one academic observer said, "White unionists can naturally be expected to resist measures that threaten their job security."[11] Six months after the Chicago protest, over 100,000 New York City construction workers demonstrated in support of the Vietnam War.[12] Participants in both demonstrations attacked bystanders. These events caused many (including me) to adopt a new perspective on white militancy: first, commentators realized that a real potential for group violence exists in the white community; and second, academicians and journalists recognized that white violence can arise from causes which are more economic than racial and be directed at targets which are not black.

Assumptions of the Research

Alvin W. Gouldner, in *The Coming Crisis of Western Sociology,* suggests that sociology transform itself by adopting a new "reflexive" posture toward itself and the material being studied. Gouldner largely restricts his discussion to sociology and social theorizing, but his ideas are equally applicable to political science and behavioral political research.

Gouldner assumes that value-free social science is impossible:

In a scientific, 'value-free' social theory, it is not that the theorist fails to situate his social objects along a good-bad dimension, but only that this assignment, having been conventionally defined as irrelevant to his task, is now defocalized and done covertly rather than being openly accomplished.[13]

A reflexive sociology would overcome the methodological dualism, inherent in today's social science, which "is based on the myth that social worlds are merely 'mirrored' in the sociologist's work, rather than seeing them as conceptually constituted by the sociologist's cognitive commitments and all his other interests."[14] In Marx's terms, Gouldner maintains that we social scientists attempt to objectify our research. Since our values inevitably influence our analysis and our conclusions, we should at the very least acknowledge our subjective relationship to the data which we study. As Gouldner says,

The social world, therefore, is to be known not simply by 'discovery' of some external fact, not only by looking outward, but also by opening oneself inward. Awareness of the *self* is seen as an indispensable avenue to awareness of the social world.[15]

Greater awareness of our relationship to the data will have two consequences. First, it will lead to even greater subjective involvement in research by encouraging the social scientist explicitly to base his research upon his own values and his own determination of what data merit his attention. This will lead the social scientist both to clarify relationships existing in the studied social world, and also to clarify and refine his own values.

A second effect of explicit subjective involvement with data is that it lays bare, both for the researcher and for the researcher's critics, the relationship between the values underlying the research and the conclusions drawn from the data. Others, and not just social scientists, will then be able to criticize and evaluate social science research.

In keeping with Gouldner's suggestions, I will specify the major assumptions underlying this book. These assumptions concern both militancy and today's political science. Some of these assumptions will be partially tested in the remaining pages. Whether tested or not, they will no doubt color my analysis and my conclusions.

Assumptions About Militancy

The research in this study is founded on the premise that the 1960's riots were essentially *political* phenomena to which specifically *political* explanations should be applied.[16] I reject Banfield's assertion that the riots represented principally "outbreaks of animal spirits and of stealing by slum dwellers."[17] I also believe that we cannot fully understand the riots through purely psychological explanations. American blacks certainly are frustrated, and these frustrations certainly led to the aggressions unleashed in the urban riots. But the source of these frustrations lies in political discontents.

I also assume that American whites are no less discontented than American blacks. Liberals have too readily pointed to white racism as lying at the base of white militancy. Many blue- and white-collar whites may be racists. Yet explaining white militancy in terms of white racism serves to mask the disadvantaged place of all too many whites in the contemporary United States. Whether racist or not, many whites, like many blacks, are the victims of a society wrought by inequalities.

Militancy[a] among blue- and white-collar whites derives from dissatisfactions with contemporary American society. Workers' dissatisfactions are two-fold: first, dissatisfactions with their relative political, economic, and status positions; and second, dissatisfactions with governmental policies. Dissatisfactions will be translated into support for militant protest activities and extreme political views. Support for militant protest and extreme political views may or may not overlap. I am thus attempting to prove that issues other than race are highly relevant to white workers. However, I have left open a possibility which I find distasteful: dissatisfactions among whites may be centered on the black community, and these dissatisfactions may be transposed into attitudes supporting violent actions against blacks.

Assumptions About Contemporary Political Science

American political science research, especially survey research on political attitudes, has been insufficiently integrated with social theorizing. Political survey researchers have not derived testable hypotheses from middle-level social theories, nor have they employed their survey results to refine such theories. Much political survey research has been atheoretical. This atheoretical approach has been deleterious for political science in general and for survey research in particular.

The use of middle-level theory in political survey research will have three advantages. First, through examining, explicating, and criticizing the theorizing of others, we will be better able to identify the assumptions and values which buttress our own research. Identifying the assumptions which limit the theorizing of others will help us to identify the assumptions which limit our own research.

Next, the application of middle-level theory will lend an historical perspective to our interpretation of survey data. The lack of an historical perspective leads political scientists to ignore a variety of interpretations for their findings. Conservatives such as Robert Nisbet, liberals such as Gunnar Myrdal, and leftists such as Norman Birnbaum and Jerzy Wiatr all charge that currently acceptable political views bias social science research.[18] The explanations which political

---

[a]In this study, militancy refers to support for political means which lie outside of "normal democratic processes." Militancy will be considered as one end of a continuum of political activities ranging from conventional to unconventional political means.

scientists seek for contemporary political phenomena tend to be those which will be accepted as politically reasonable rather than scorned as politically outlandish. This represents a particularly severe problem in political survey research, where the choice and framing of the research questions heavily influence the findings. The employment of middle-level theory will aid political scientists in formulating research questions which are not heavily biased by popular, possibly opportunistic interpretations of recent events. The application of middle-level theory makes it possible to recognize and to test alternate explanations of current political phenomena.

The lack of an historical perspective in political survey research also takes another form. Too many political scientists fail to "take account of the *historical character* of the facts."[19] Survey researchers should realize that facts change: a survey conducted in 1970 may uncover attitudes which are peculiar to that year. As W.G. Runciman points out, " . . . the techniques of the sample survey are useful only if they are the servants and not the masters of historical interpretation."[20] Examining middle-level theory will help political scientists to derive hypotheses and explanations of survey findings which are less historically-specific, and which reveal relationships between present and past events.

Third, the utilization of middle-level theory will lead to a truly cumulative political science. The absence of theoretical underpinnings in political surveys has resulted in research which has been cumulative primarily in its methodological advances and in its construction of low-level theories. These advances, however, have been made largely at the expense of refinements in middle-level theory. Survey research presents political scientists with opportunities to expand upon, correct, and refine broader theories of political behavior. Yet researchers who have employed surveys in this manner have been more the exception than the rule.[21]

Aims of the Research

I will use a variety of methods to explain white militancy in 1970 Boston. In Chapter 1 I will briefly delineate a Marxian framework and Marxian questions which can be used in studying the 1960's black riots and white militancy. In Chapter 2 this framework will be utilized to identify the unstated assumptions of those who have conducted survey research on militancy, and the ways in which those assumptions have limited the utility of those surveys. Chapter 3 centers on building a broad theoretical framework for studying white militancy. To do this, I will specify and remedy the conceptual weaknesses in Marx's theorizing. Drawing upon both a Marxian-Weberian theoretical backdrop and the empirical findings of current studies on black and white militancy, I will then establish my own theory of dissatisfactions and militancy. Chapters 4 and 5 contain an empirical examination of hypotheses derived from my theory of militancy and dissatisfactions. After applying these hypotheses to 1970 survey data on Boston white men, I will then employ the data analysis to refine both my own theoretical framework and Marx's (Chapter 6).

Acknowledgments

Many friends helped to make this a better book. Desmond Ellis of York University contributed to the early conceptualization of the research; Lou Lipsitz and Thad Beyle, both of the University of North Carolina, David Vogler, of Wheaton College, and Harvey Klehr, of Emory University, all read, commented on, and criticized various drafts; Norman Kurtz of Brandeis University provided helpful methodological hints. Janice Neely and Lillian Myers of O.S.T.I. patiently persisted in the preparation of the final typescript. Research grants from the National Science Foundation enabled me to conduct the survey which forms the basis of Chapters 4, 5, and 6. Finally, a special thanks to Gerald Wright of Florida Atlantic University, who generously provided advice concerning data manipulation. Any shortcomings or strange ideas contained in the following pages are mine alone.

1

Marx's Questions About Militancy

Sometimes Mrs. Turpin occupied herself at night naming the classes of people. On the bottom of the heap were most colored people, not the kind she would have been if she had been one, but most of them; then next to them – not above, just away from – were the white trash; then above them were the home-owners, and above them the home-and-land owners, to which she and Claud belonged. Above she and Claud were people with a lot of money and much bigger houses and much more land. But here the complexity of it would begin to bear in on her, for some of the people with a lot of money were common and ought to be below she and Claud and some of the people who had good blood had lost their money and had to rent and then there were colored people who owned their homes and land as well. There was a colored dentist in town who had two red Lincolns and a swimming pool and a farm with registered whiteface cattle on it. Usually by the time she had fallen asleep all the classes of people were moiling and roiling around in her head, and she would dream they were all crammed in together in a box car, being ridden off to be put in a gas oven. [1]

Flannery O'Connor

Class, Consciousness, and Action

If Marx were alive today, what questions would he ask about black and white militancy? How would Marx analyze the recent riots? If Marx, instead of gathering survey data in 1880 on the French working class, had attempted a similar survey in 1972 on America's black and white working class, what research questions would he pose? [2] Marx's forty years of written work provide tentative answers to these questions. In investigating black and white militancy in today's United States, Marx would focus upon three areas: the objective class structure of the United States, subjective class consciousness, and political action arising from subjective class consciousness.

Objective Class Structure [a]

Current interpreters of Marx, such as C. Wright Mills and Ralf Dahrendorf,

---

[a]Great difficulties have been caused by the semantic confusion of Marx's differentiation between those factors which define an individual's position in the class structure, and those factors which lead to class consciousness and political action. In this work, "objective class" will refer to structural classes, and "subjective class" to psychological classes.

1

misrepresent Marx's thought by maintaining that he views capitalist class structures in revolutionary and pre-revolutionary situations as structurally polarized.[3] In the minds of Mills and Dahrendorf, Marx would have maintained that the 1960's riots resulted from a structural bipolarization of American objective classes: a productive working class, composed largely of black workers, revolted against an unproductive middle class, composed mostly of whites. Such an interpretation does grave damage to Marx's theorizing, and is based upon four misreadings of his work.

Misreading Number One – Due to the inevitable cycles of the capitalist economy, the number of workers increases, while their income and standard of living decline.

Misreading Number Two – A decrease in the number of those benefiting from the workers' labors accompanies the increasing hardship of an ever increasing portion of the populace.

Misreading Number Three – Greater reliance on machinery results in larger work places, more concentrated capital, and expanded profits for the few remaining capitalists. Former capitalists and members of the middle class become proletarians.

Misreading Number Four – And, so the argument continues, a communist revolution can occur only in advanced capitalist societies where workers are impoverished and the class structure is polarized. A revolutionary situation thus presupposes two classes, and two classes only: the impoverished workers and the rich capitalists.

If Karl Marx had based his theorizing on these four points, any application of his theories to current American militancy would be useless: the wages of the American working man continually increase, while at the same time the American middle class grows in size. Yet Marx's theorizing on the objective class structure is applicable to the U.S.A. – and it is applicable precisely because he correctly predicted those changes in capitalist societies which would lead to higher wages and a continuous objective class structure composed of numerous, closely connected segments. To support this view, we must investigate two themes in Marx's theorizing: first, his thoughts on the changing conditions of the working class; and second, his writings on the growing middle class in advanced capitalist societies.

The United States which was rent by the 1960's riots is one of the world's richest nations. True, this wealth is unevenly distributed; and true, to the millions of blacks and whites living below the poverty level, the gross wealth of our nation is an irrelevant, harshly mocking fact. But despite the massive inequalities inherent in the American economic structure, the bulk of this country's working class earns more than ever before in our two hundred year history.

Marx maintains that the general lot of the worker inevitably worsens, and that a revolutionary situation presupposes maximum discontent among the workers. Could Marx have believed that the United States of the 1960's and

1970's — the United States in which workers, black and white alike, were earning more than ever before — would be convulsed by revolutionary riots? The answer is *yes*. Three clues exist to this unexpected turn in Marx's thought.

The first clue lies in Marx's theorizing on the continual increase in human needs. Throughout his writing career, Marx repeatedly asserts that human needs increase as the means of production become modernized: " . . . as soon as a need is satisfied, . . . new needs are made. . . ."[4] Human needs reflect the contemporary culture, and these needs expand as the culture defines new needs as necessary to existence.

American capitalists will pay only those wages which are necessary for maintaining the workers' subsistence level and for attracting workers in a competitive labor market. Yet the minimum subsistence level of the nineteenth century American worker differs from the minimum subsistence level of the twentieth century American worker. The nineteenth century capitalist paid wages that barely included such needs as food, clothing, and housing. The twentieth century, with changes in the means of production, has brought on an expansion of workers' needs. The contemporary American capitalist often pays wages that meet a subsistence level consisting of such needs as televisions and automobiles.

A second clue can be found in Marx's conception of the relationship between the workers' and the capitalists' standards of living. In a series of articles appearing in *Neue Rheinische Zeitung* during 1849, Marx indicates that the worker's satisfaction with his standard of living is determined not only by culturally imposed and thus relative needs, but also by comparison of his standard of living to that of the capitalists:

An appreciable rise in wages presupposes a rapid growth of productive capital. Rapid growth of productive capital calls forth just as rapid a growth of wealth, of luxury, of social needs and social pleasures. Therefore, although the pleasures of the labourer have increased, the social gratification which they afford has fallen in comparison with the increased pleasures of the capitalist, which are inaccessible to the worker, in comparison with the stage of development of society in general. Our wants and pleasures have their origin in society; we therefore measure them in relation to society; we do not measure them in relation to the objects which serve for their gratification. Since they are of a social nature, they are of a relative nature.[5]

In *Capital* Marx incorporates this distinction between absolute and relative increases into his discussion of workers' wages: "if the working class has remained 'poor,' only 'less poor' in proportion as it produces for the wealthy class 'an intoxicating augmentation of wealth and power,' then it has remained relatively just as poor. If the extremes of poverty have not lessened, they have increased, because the extremes of wealth have."[6] Workers' wages and their standard of living may increase absolutely. Yet every time the workers' wages go up, the profits garnered by the capitalists grow even larger. The decline in wages is not absolute, but relative to the increasing profits won by the capitalists.

The third and final clue to Marx's belief in the betterment of the worker's standard of living is inherent in his discussions of the nature of capitalism. Whenever Marx speaks of wage increases, he also specifies that "the more or less favourable circumstances in which the wage-working class supports and multiplies itself, in no way alter the fundamental character of capitalist production. . . ."[7] the rise of wages therefore is confined within limits that not only leave intact the foundations of the capitalistic system, but also secure its reproduction on a progressive scale."[8] Any increase in workers' wages will not rectify a major fault of the capitalist economy: alienation.[9]

Even though Marx sagely foresaw an increase in working class wages, this does not mean that he necessarily correctly predicted the American class structure which was so vigorously attacked during the 1960's riots. Rather than starkly polarized between the two extremes of many bone-poor proletarians and few fat-cat capitalists, the United States' objective class structure possesses both a large working class and a large middle class. Many would have us believe that the size of the American middle class disproves Marx's predictions, while proving once and for all that Marxian theorizing cannot be reasonably applied to the United States.

A large and growing middle class represents an integral part of Marx's mature thought on the evolution of objective class structures in advanced capitalist societies. In his 1848 call to arms, *The Communist Manifesto,* Marx does assert that capitalist "society as a whole is more and more splitting up into two great hostile camps, into two great classes directly facing each other: Bourgeoisie and Proletariat."[10] In this same dramatic work, Marx goes on to indicate that classes standing between the capitalists and the workers, and those capitalists who have lost their ill-won wealth, will "sink gradually into the proletariat"[11] and "decay and finally disappear in the face of modern industry."[12] In *Capital* Marx continues to predict a decrease in the size of the capitalist class: ". . . the larger capitals beat the smaller. . . . Competition. . . . always ends in the ruin of many small capitalists, whose capitals partly pass into the hands of their conquerors, partly vanish."[13] Is Marx making the same prediction in *Capital* as he made almost twenty years earlier in the *Manifesto?* No, for in *Capital* Marx maintains that capitalist class castoffs will not necessarily leave the broader middle class.

Throughout the 1850's and 1860's Marx admits that former members of the capitalist and self-employed lower middle classes form a distinct segment which falls economically between the productive working class and the unproductive capitalist middle class.[14] Marx implies that the developing structural middle ground consists of two broad occupational categories. The first category derives from "entirely new branches of production . . . [which are] creating new fields of labor. . . ."[15] Marx maintains that there will be a ". . . class of persons, whose occupation it is to look after the whole of the machinery and repair it from time to time; such as engineers, [and] mechanics. . . . This is a superior class of workmen, some of them scientifically educated, others brought up to a trade; it is distinct from the factory operative class. . . ."[16] The second broad category contains salesmen, clerks, capitalist middlemen, and a variety of other occupations, such as government officials and lawyers, that Marx terms "ideological" workers.[17]

Marx's structural middle ground bears similarities to both the working class and the capitalist class. Like the workers, members of this new middle class neither own the means of production nor control the products of their labor. Like the capitalists, they perform no productive work, but rather live by dealing in the products of working class labor.

If Karl Marx were alive today, he would *not* begin investigating black and white militancy by asking: "are there only two principal objective classes in the United States?" Marx would expect to see, and would readily recognize, a large middle class consisting of diverse internal segments including capitalists and landowners, commercial middlemen such as clerks and salesmen, and skilled technicians.[18] Similarly, Marx would anticipate a working class consisting of both the productive workers themselves and unemployed workers – the "industrial reserve army;"[19] he would not be surprised when someone told him that many members of the working class earn no less than lower middle class members. As in the nineteenth century, he would also puzzle over the farmers, many of whom he would expect to see being pushed off their farmlands by the steady growth of profit-hungry agribusiness.[20] Finally, Marx would once again scoff at the lumpenproletariat underclass composed of "vagabonds," "swindlers," "mountebanks," and "beggars."[21]

Subjective Class Consciousness

Marx, then, does not predict a structural bipolarization of objective classes in the United States. Yet one would be both foolhardy and wrong to assert that Marx would fail to posit some sort of polarization among the objective classes existing in the contemporary United States. If Marx today sat down to write a work on American black and white militancy, he would probably entitle it "Class Struggles in the United States, 1964-1972." In analyzing white and black militancy, Marx would undoubtedly stress class polarization. But Marx would argue that the precondition for a revolutionary situation is not a polarization of objective class structure; rather, the precondition for a revolutionary situation is a polarization of subjective class consciousness. The nature and ingredients of subjective class consciousness represent the most important predictor of whether or not a revolutionary situation will emerge.[b] Recent black riots resulted more from subjective class polarization between black and white consciousnesses than from objective class divisions between America's black and white communities.

Marx differentiates objective from subjective classes in his frequently

---

[b]Marx sees three factors as facilitating the growth of subjective class consciousness: first, the expansion of nationally based capitalist economies to include a world-market; second, the absence of intraclass cultural divisions; and third, horizontal communications among members of the same objective class.

repeated distinction between a "class in itself" and a "class for itself." In the *Poverty of Philosophy,* Marx writes:

Economic conditions had first transformed the mass of the people of the country into workers. The combination of capital has created for this mass a common situation, common interests. This mass is thus already a class as against capital, but not yet for itself. In the struggle . . . this mass becomes united, and constitutes itself as a class for itself. The interests it defends become class interests.[22]

According to Marx, a class in itself occupies a position in the objective class structure. Broadly speaking, a class in itself consists of "millions of families [living] . . . under economic conditions of existence that separate their mode of life, their interests and their culture from those of the other classes. . . ."[23] More narrowly, a class in itself is composed of a large group which shares common characteristics in terms of: ownership (or nonownership) of the means of production; control (or lack of control) over the products of their labor; and productivity (or unproductivity) of their work.

A class for itself is composed of members of an objective class who have joined together after recognizing their common position and their common interests. To paraphrase Marx's discussion of the French peasantry in *The Eighteenth Brumaire,* an objective class – a class in itself – becomes transformed into a subjective class – a class for itself – when its members possess more than "merely a local interconnection" and when "the identity of their interests" begets both community and political organization.[24] A class in itself is thus a structural grouping based upon a shared economic situation, while a class for itself is an attitudinal grouping based upon shared beliefs. Most American blacks clearly fall within the working class – "a class in itself." Yet the 1960's riots emerged out of "a class for itself" – blacks who had recognized their common interests against white merchants and policemen.

A class for itself, in Marx's terms, is nearly synonymous with a class that has attained class consciousness. Surprisingly, Marx only obliquely defines the ingredients of class consciousness. In 1844, Marx points out that "for *one* class to be the liberating class *par excellence,* it is necessary that another class should be openly the oppressing class."[25] Marx thus intimates that one ingredient of class consciousness is the perception of one class as an oppressive force. Five years later, Marx expands upon this notion:

A house may be large or small; as long as the neighbouring houses are likewise small, it satisfies all social requirements for a residence. But let there arise next to the little house a palace, and the little house shrinks into a hut. The little house now makes it clear that its inmate has no social position at all to maintain, or but a very insignificant one; and however high it may shoot up in the course of civilisation, if the neighbouring palace rises in equal or even in greater measure, the occupant of the relatively little house will always find himself more uncomfortable, more dissatisfied, more cramped within his four walls.[26]

Marx thereby implies that another ingredient of class consciousness is awareness of an individual's relative position in the objective class structure. Inferring from these passages, class consciousness can be defined as both awareness of the nature of the objective class structure, and awareness of the individual's own objective position in the class structure relative to that of other classes.

Who attains subjective class consciousness? Is subjective class consciousness restricted to working class blacks and whites or are they just more likely to become class conscious than middle class blacks and whites? Would Marx have agreed with Marcuse's statement that "the revolution was to be the direct organized action of the *proletariat as a class* − or it was not at all"?[27]

Marx argues that an all-transforming revolution must be led by "a sphere of society which has a universal character because its sufferings are universal, and which does not claim a *particular redress* because the wrong which is done to it is not a *particular wrong* but *wrong in general.*"[28] This "sphere of society" is, of course, the working class.

Yet Marx also maintains that individual members of other objective classes can attain class consciousness: ". . . it is again nonsense to say that they, together with the bourgeoisie, and with the feudal lords into the bargain, 'form only one reactionary mass' in relation to the working class."[29] Some poor farmers and lower middle class members will become class conscious through recognizing their own structural position and interests as distinct from those of the capitalists. Others will become conscious "through the contemplation of the situation" of the working class.[30]

The all-transforming revolution must be based upon a unified subjective class. This subjective class, however, is an attitudinal grouping consisting primarily of working class members, but also including members of other objective classes. Contrary to Ossowski's interpretation, the revolutionary class structure consists of several objective classes but only two subjective classes.[31] Marx makes this point particularly well in his works dealing with French civil strife. In *Class Struggles in France,* he comments: "so swiftly had the march of the revolution ripened conditions, that the friends of reform of all shades, the most moderate claims of the middle classes, were compelled to group themselves round the banner of the most extreme party of revolution, round the red flag."[32] In *Eighteenth Brumaire* Marx adds that ". . . the peasants find their natural ally and leader in the *urban proletariat*. . . ."[33]

Writing today, Marx would once again stress the all-important role of the urban proletariat in black and white militancy. He would hypothesize that big-city blacks would be most aware of their own position in the objective class structure relative to other classes, and he would correctly predict that the urban black working class forms the vanguard of black militancy. He would hypothesize that big-city white workers would be acutely aware of their relative standing and that they would be more militant than other whites. Yet Marx, in asking questions about militancy and subjective class consciousness, would also concern himself with middle class members. Rather than assuming that no middle class members would attain revolutionary subjective class consciousness, Marx would question the white and black bourgeoisie to discover what factors motivated some of them to become class conscious militants, and what led others to oppose the subjectively conscious working class. Lastly, Marx would bristle at those who arbitrarily differentiate class consciousness among whites from class consciousness among blacks, and white militancy from black militancy. In Marx's mind, class consciousness among both whites and blacks would be cut from the same cloth: the recognition that others occupy relatively higher positions in the objective class structure, and the realization that this relative gap ever increases.

Political Action

Throughout the 1960's, criticism of Dr. Martin Luther King's Southern Christian Leadership Conference increased. Even though America's blacks had more respect for King the man than for any other American public figure, many became dissatisfied with his tactic of "nonviolent confrontation."[34] Denounced as go-slow and ineffective, King's tactics were abandoned by many younger black leaders. Such blacks, ranging from New York City's Bronx High School of Science-educated Stokely Carmichael to California's Folsom Prison-interned Eldridge Cleaver, soon endorsed violent tactics which they regarded as more likely to bring about rapid change. Many commentators and public officials denounced the guns of Carmichael and Cleaver as revolutionary, and applauded the sit-ins of King and Abernathy as acceptably liberal.

What would Marx have said? Would Marx have regarded the black violence of the 1960's as truly revolutionary, and rejected the black nonviolence of earlier years as too liberal and counter-revolutionary? What tactics would Marx recommend to foment revolution in the United States of today?

Marx sets forth three criteria for truly revolutionary action. First, an action is truly revolutionary only if it brings about change throughout an entire society; any action which affects only a limited geographic or economic portion of society is not truly revolutionary.[35] A second criterion for truly revolutionary action is that it must involve both economic and more narrow political change. The 1776 American Colonies' break with the British represented a "bourgeois" and not a "true" revolution, for the Americans, while interested in establishing a more egalitarian political structure, were not concerned with restructuring the capitalist division of labor. Third, truly revolutionary action must have a broad participatory and supportive base in a subjective class. As Marx points out in his 1871 letter to Bolte, ". . . out of the separate economic movements of the workers there grows up everywhere a *political* movement, that is to say a movement of the *class,* with the object of achieving its interests in a general form, in a form possessing a general social form of compulsion."[36] Marx rejects the seemingly political actions of more narrowly based groups. In Marx's view, groups with narrow supportive bases can achieve only the overthrow of a particular regime or form of government, and not any more lasting and fundamental change in the division of labor and the objective class structure.[37]

What actions meet these three criteria? What constitutes revolutionary political action? In Marx's eyes, is King or Cleaver a revolutionary? Marx's answers lie in his thoughts on peaceful and violent change.

In the 1840's Marx repeatedly rejects the possibility of nonviolent revolutionary change. At the end of *The Poverty of Philosophy,* he admiringly quotes George Sand's harsh words: "Combat or death: Bloody struggle or extinction. It is thus that the question is inexorably put."[38] But during the next three decades, Marx becomes increasingly sympathetic to the idea of peaceful change. Immediately before the formation of the Paris Commune in 1870, Marx exhorts French workers: "The French workmen must perform their duties as citizens. . . . Let them calmly and resolutely improve the opportunities of republican liberty, for the work of their own class organisation."[39] Addressing the 1872 Congress of the First International, Marx says: ". . . we do not deny that there are countries like England and America and if I am familiar with your institutions, Holland, where labour may attain its goal by peaceful means."[40] Contrary to the interpretations of Lichtheim and Lipset, the Hague speech and other similar statements do not represent a basic change in Marx's concept of revolutionary political action.[41] In the 1840's Marx concluded that only group based violence met his three criteria of revolutionary action. Later in his life Marx decided that in certain countries group actions other than violence met those criteria too. Marx never rejects violence.[42] Rather, he broadens his concept of which acts meet his criteria of revolutionary political activity. In his mature thought Marx sees political action as a continuous variable ranging from peaceful to violent acts. No point along the continuum is inherently preferable; the determination of the propriety of a particular act is made by judging the situation in a particular country at a particular time.[43]

Violence, in Marx's eyes, is neither moral nor immoral, neither revolutionary nor counter-revolutionary. Workers in some countries can achieve revolutionary ends through violence. However, violence must meet the criteria for revolutionary action: it must aim at bringing about change throughout an entire society; it must involve both economic and more narrow political change; and it must possess a broad participatory and supportive base in a subjective class. Violence which meets these criteria is truly political and revolutionary; hence it is justifiable and moral. Violence which does not meet the criteria is neither revolutionary nor justifiable.

Returning to the black and white militancy of the 1960's and 1970's, we would once again find Karl Marx applying his three criteria to assess and evaluate the divergent tactics employed by King and Cleaver. When asked for advice on what actions should be taken to further the black revolution, Marx would answer the query with three rhetorical questions: What tactic would bring about change throughout *all* segments of American society?; What tactic would lead to both economic and more narrow political change?; What tactic would gain the most support and participation within the subjective working class?

Marx and Militancy: Some Questions

Writing today, Marx would adopt a familiar framework with which to evaluate and research militancy among America's whites and blacks. Critics would maintain that Marx's framework is too simplistic, and that it displays only a glancing familiarity with the exceptional problems of the U.S.A. Marx would quickly reply that although individual advanced capitalist countries do indeed differ from each other in many ways, they also share important similarities. Marx would assert that adopting an analytic framework which is peculiar to the U.S.A. of today leads social scientists to overlook many possible explanations of militancy.

In evaluating white militancy, Marx would stress three central ideas which emerge from his theorizing:

First, white dissatisfactions are not generically different from black dissatisfactions. The same motive force lies behind both white and black dissatisfactions: subjective class consciousness, defined by Marx as the extent to which a person perceives a gap between his own subjective position and those at the top of the class structure. The size of the perceived gap will influence the person's views on both economic and more narrow political change. Marx thus implies that an individual's economic beliefs overlap with his political beliefs, and both are determined by his class dissatisfactions.

In Marx's view, the objective class position of an individual only partially determines his subjective class identification and his dissatisfaction with his position in the class structure. However, those people with similar perceptions of their class situation will bear greater attitudinal similarities to each other than they will to others who, even though their positions in the objective class structure may be similar, differ in their subjective class identification. Subjective class identification is of greater import in determining attitudes than objective class position.

Second, the use of violent political means, in and of itself, is neither revolutionary nor radical. Political means lie on a continuum of political actions, ranging from wholly conventional, peaceful acts to unconventional, violent acts. Any person's choice of a particular means will be determined by strictly utilitarian considerations: Will the act achieve the desired end?; Will other people support and endorse the act?

Marx thus avers that a person's choice of militant, violent means tells us nothing about his choice of political ends. A white leftist may choose peaceful means because he feels that peaceful means alone will successfully achieve revolutionary ends in the United States; a white rightist might choose violent, militant means because he calculates that only through the use of militant means will he attain his own counter-revolutionary goals. Similarly, knowing that a person is subjectively class conscious tells us nothing about his choice of militant or nonmilitant means. Militant means can be employed as tactics for both maintaining and improving one's position in the objective class structure. Militancy and radicalism are conceptually and empirically distinct from each other.

Radical ends and militant means may or may not overlap. Militant means can thus be directed at a wide variety of targets, including both the government and other social groups. The leftist white militant might target his violence against the government; the rightist white militant might target his violence against those social groups which opt for radical leftist changes in American society.

Third, Marx would have us believe that white hostility towards blacks reflects basic dissatisfactions among whites with their place in the objective class structure. Marx thus focuses attention on white dissatisfactions with the socio-political structure, *not* on white prejudice toward blacks.

2 Marx and Survey Research on Militancy

Pa said, "S'pose he's tellin' the truth—that fella?"

The preacher answered, "He's tellin' the truth, awright. The truth for him. He wasn't makin' nothin' up."

"How about us?" Tom demanded. "Is that the truth for us?"

"I don' know," said Casy.[a]

John Steinbeck

In research the answers one gets depend in part on the kinds of questions he asks.[1]

V.O. Key and Frank Munger

Introduction

The political scientist employing a middle-level theoretical framework derived from Marx would ask the following questions about contemporary white and black militancy:

Are political means regarded as being on a continuum, or do people see conventional political means as generically different from unconventional political means?

Does support for militant means overlap with support for any particular political or economic ends?

Do black militancy and white militancy arise from the same sources?

Do people who perceive militant means as effective and who are also leftist radicals (perceive their subjective class position as low) target their violence against the government? Are they more willing to support militant means than others who are also leftist radicals and who perceive their subjective class position as low, but who do not regard violence as effective?

Do whites who perceive militant means as effective and who are also conservatives (perceive their subjective class position as high) target their violence against those groups, such as blacks, which they see as threatening their privileged position within American society?

13

As will become clear below, the atheoretical perspective of all too many political survey researchers blinded them to these questions.

The functions of a middle-level theory include encouraging the questioning of political and theoretical assumptions lying behind research designs; raising research questions which are not biased by currently popular interpretations of recent events; promoting clear conceptualization of individual variables within research designs; and providing a set of interrelated hypotheses for testing. The lack of a shared middle-level theoretical framework in black and white militancy studies has led to unasked questions, unwarranted assumptions, and inadequate conceptualization of individual variables.

Survey Literature on Black and White Militancy

Surveys on Black Militancy: Emphases and Findings[2]

Several sociologists have drawn attention to the assumptions lying behind recent research on black militancy. Allen D. Grimshaw draws attention to the implications of differing assumptions about riots in his 1967 paper, "Three Views of Urban Violence: Civil Disturbance, Racial Revolt, Class Assault."[3] Grimshaw, however, limits his fine critique to journalistic and political interpretations of the 1960's black riots. James A. Geschwender, in his 1968 article "Civil Rights Protest and Riots: A Disappearing Distinction," attempts a similar analysis of academic interpretations of black rioting. Geschwender reinterprets survey findings on riot participants, and questions the basis upon which "a number of social scientists . . . view civil rights activities and riots as two different and contradictory types of phenomena."[4]

The numerous surveys on black militancy, which extend back to Kenneth Clark's study of attitudinal support for the 1943 Harlem riot,[5] can be categorized into three groups by virtue of the authors' theoretical foci and independent variables.[b] These studies all share a common dependent variable: endorsement/participation/support for violence, militancy, or riots emanating from blacks and directed at whites, property, or governmental surrogates. It should be noted that although most authors assume that targets are selected because of racial considerations, they do not impute purely racial causes to black militancy.

The first group of studies have as their emphasis perceived social and political structural inadequacies as the cause of black militancy. The conceptualization and measurement of perceived structural inadequacies vary. Schwartz, and Sears and McConahay employ political alienation and political disaffection to measure the person's perception of structural failings. Although Schwartz discovers no

---

[b]Several studies include a variety of independent variables; where important and appropriate, these studies will be placed in more than one category.

direct relationship between political alienation and militancy, Sears and McConahay demonstrate that those who were most politically disaffected were most likely to have participated in the Watts riot.[6] Closely related to this finding are the results on political distrust reported by Sears and McConahay, using data from the UCLA riot study, by Paige, relying on Kerner Commission Newark data, and by Aberbach and Walker. These investigators discover strong relationships between political distrust and riot support; blacks who trust American government and public officials the least are most likely to endorse and participate in riots.[7]

Other researchers use relative deprivation as the framework for measuring perceived social and political structural inadequacies. Singer and his colleagues point out that a higher proportion of those arrested for participation in the 1967 Detroit riot than those in a riot zone sample ". . . perceived that their conditions had worsened within the past few years. . . .;" Caplan and Paige, however, find no such difference between Newark rioters and Newark nonrioters.[8] Turning to more specific structural inadequacies, Wellstone concludes that perceived relative deprivation concerning both treatment by whites and influence over governmental decisions is strongly related to militancy; Ransford similarly uncovers a strong relationship between Los Angeles blacks' dissatisfaction with their treatment as compared to other reference groups and their willingness to use violence. Caplan and Paige also report that Newark rioters were more likely than other respondents to believe that the economic gap between rich and poor blacks was increasing.[9] Regarding work dissatisfaction, Caplan and Paige, as well as Sears and McConahay, discover that blacks who were most dissatisfied with their present jobs — and blacks with the highest job aspirations — were most militant.[10] Finally, Murphy and Watson discover that consumer discontent was most frequent among those who supported and participated in the Watts riot.[11]

A second group of survey researchers focus upon political beliefs as a cause of black militancy. Hahn, and Murphy and Watson assert that black militants are likely to distrust local police.[12] Moore, Sears and McConahay, and Hahn also deal with the relationship between satisfaction with more general local government policy outputs and militancy. These studies, although not directly comparable, do provide a surprising contrast: Hahn, and Sears and McConahay show that blacks who are dissatisfied with local government outputs most strongly support rioting; Moore, however, finds that dissatisfaction with postriot governmental outputs in Winston-Salem is unrelated to a projective militancy scale of protest activities and to actual participation in postriot protest activities.[13]

In the third and final group of surveys on black militancy, researchers utilize demographic measures as major independent variables. These measures, especially education and occupation, could be interpreted as rough and indirect indicators of a person's power in the socio-political structure. Such studies produce interesting and conflicting results. The Kerner Commission, Clark,

Wellstone, Schulman, and Marx find that the better educated are more militant.[14] Among those arrested for participation in the Detroit riot, Singer, Osborn, and Geschwender demonstrate, "there is a positive relationship between level of educational attainment and seriousness of charge."[15] Campbell and Schuman, and Murphy and Watson, on the other hand, report no clear relationship between education and militancy.[16]

When these authors turn to occupation as their independent variable, the data are less consistent. Marx discovers that blacks with higher status occupations are more militant; Caplan and Paige, on the other hand, assert that Newark blacks with unskilled jobs were more likely to have participated in the 1967 riot. To add to the confusion, Murphy and Watson's Los Angeles data show that blacks with semiskilled jobs are more likely to have rioted than either those with unskilled jobs or those with skilled and white-collar jobs.[17] One somewhat consistent finding does emerge from these data: in both Newark and Los Angeles, unemployed blacks were slightly more likely to have rioted.[18]

Surveys on White Militancy: Emphases and Findings

Few surveys dealing with white militancy have been conducted. The major investigations were counterparts to surveys of black rioting; Campbell and Schuman's 1968 15-city study was sponsored by the Kerner Commission, and Morris and Jeffries' 1965 survey was conducted as part of the UCLA Los Angeles Riot Study. Undertaken during a time when black riots were a reality and white reaction a much feared possibility, studies of white militant reaction to black rioting have little in common with studies of black militancy. Investigators of white counter-violence have shown less concern than those investigating black violence with employing or testing theoretical frameworks. The absence of theoretical frameworks has had unfortunate consequences for research designs and findings: while students of black violence focus substantial attention on black dissatisfactions with political and social structural in-adequacies, as well as unfair distributions of governmental outputs, students of white reactions to black violence pay less attention to these causal factors.

In addition to surveys partially focussing on antiblack militancy among whites, other researchers delve into antigovernmental militancy. Antigovern-mental militancy surveys differ in important ways from surveys including questions on violent retaliation against blacks. Most significantly, those conducting antigovernmental militancy surveys were primarily interested in militancy as a means of achieving social change and redressing governmental injustices; race relations and antiblack militancy are only tangentially covered in these surveys. One set of surveys tells us about white violence towards blacks, while the other tells us about white violence towards the government. No one survey tells us fully about both, and no one survey tells us if the factors which lead whites violently to oppose blacks also lead whites violently to oppose the government. Another difference between the two sets of surveys lies in the manner in which scholars operationally define militancy. While the antiblack militancy surveys queried respondents about using violence to retaliate against black rioters, the antigovernmental militancy surveys focus upon projective situations, in which respondents were asked to imagine what they would do if ". . . Congress has just passed a law prohibiting anyone from saying anything against the government."[19] Other antigovernmental militancy surveys center on the respondent's judgment of whether violence is necessary for social change, or whether the respondent believes that people unfairly treated by the government can justifiably engage in a variety of militant protest activities. Because of this great variation in the definition and operationalization of militancy, comparing findings proves difficult.

Let us now compare studies of white militancy with those of black militancy, using the same categories based on principal theoretical foci and independent variables. A large group of surveys on black militancy and rioting deal with perceived structural inadequacies, operationalized in terms of political alienation, political disaffection, lack of economic mobility, job discontent, and consumer dissatisfaction. In studies of whites, few such questions were raised. Campbell reports the limited number of comparable findings: whites who are very dissatisfied with their income and their housing are most likely to condone counter-rioting against blacks.[20] With this single exception, we political survey researchers failed to ask whether white reaction to black rioting reflects basic white discontent with inadequacies and inequalities in the American socio-political structure.

Turning to studies of antigovernmental militancy among whites, we find more attention focused on one particular aspect of perceived social and political structural inadequacies: political powerlessness. Olsen, in his 1965 survey consisting almost entirely of white Ann Arbor residents, finds that people who believe that they have little political power are most likely to disapprove of militant antigovernmental protest. Schwartz's investigation of white attitudes toward the Newark public schools yields different results; he finds no direct relationship between political alienation and endorsement of militant tactics to induce change in the local schools.[21] The differing results, while not readily explicable, may result from the dissimilar definitions of militancy: Olsen's questions about approval of protest probably tap a civil libertarian dimension; while Schwartz's questions, asked in a riot-torn city and specific to the racially charged public school issue, may draw upon white fears of racial unrest.

If social scientists give little attention to perceived structural inadequacies as a cause of white militancy, they give only slightly more attention to political beliefs as a possible motive force leading to white violence. Campbell demonstrates that whites who oppose black protest, civil rights legislation, and federal aid to cities more strongly endorse white counter-rioting.[22] Jeffries, Turner, and Morris report comparable findings; Los Angeles whites who unsympathetically define the 1965 Watts riot were more likely to have considered using guns to protect themselves against black rioters.[23]

These data seem to indicate that the potential white counter-rioter bears little political similarity to his black counterpart: while black militants distrust government because they feel that they receive few benefits from it, white militants oppose that very legislation which blacks want strengthened. The black militant appears revolutionary, and the antiblack militant appears counter-revolutionary. Yet additional data reported by Campbell from the Kerner Commission 15-city study cast doubt on this facile characterization. Like black rioters, whites who endorse counter-rioting are most likely to feel dissatisfied with their mayor and with community services tendered by their city government. Here we have the first major indication of common cause for black and white militancy — and that common cause lies in biracial dissatisfaction with local government.[24]

The fullest data in white militancy studies center on the association between demographic variables and willingness to use political violence. In some black militancy surveys, a weak positive correlation exists between education and militancy: better educated blacks support rioting and militant protest more strongly than poorly educated blacks. Yet when we look at militant white reaction to black rioting, the opposite relationship emerges: Morris and Jeffries, in their investigation of Los Angeles whites, and Campbell and Schuman, in their 15-city study, all discover that college educated whites are *least* willing violently to retaliate against black rioters.[25] As we will see in a later chapter, one plausible explanation for this discrepancy between white and black militancy lies in the threat posed to working class, poorly educated whites by black advances. Some support for this explanation can be found by looking at the relationship between white occupational status and white militancy. Although the results are by no means overwhelmingly clear, both the 15-city and the Los Angeles data do hint that whites with blue-collar occupations are slightly more likely militantly to oppose black rioters than are whites with white-collar occupations.[26] Further support for our racial threat explanation emerges from surveys dealing with antigovernmental militancy among whites. Levy, using data from a 1968 survey conducted for the National Commission on the Causes and Consequences of Violence, and Olsen, in his Ann Arbor survey, both find that poorly educated whites most strongly disapprove of militant protest against governmental injustice, and well-educated whites most strongly support antigovernmental militancy; Olsen also finds that whites with white-collar jobs are more likely to support antigovernmental militancy.[27]

Different data from different surveys seem to indicate that antiblack militancy and antigovernmental militancy represent starkly different phenomena, with dramatically different causes. Antiblack militancy, apparently most prevalent within the white working class, may result from fear of black advances which threaten the already tenuous position of blue-collar whites; antigovernmental militancy, strongest among better educated whites with white-collar occupations, cannot be similarly explained. Yet since no one study has explicated the causes of both antigovernmental and antiblack militancy and since different studies define antiblack militancy and antigovernmental militancy differently, we cannot answer an all-important question: Do antiblack militancy and antigovernmental militancy result from different factors? Answering this question will be the task of Chapters 5 and 6.

Marx's Challenge to the Empirical Answers

Do white and black militancy surveys answer Marx's questions? These surveys provide some answers and some hints of answers. But to uncover the answers and the hints, we must search through a plethora of studies with widely disparate theoretical, conceptual, and operational foci. What questions are answered? What questions remain? And why do the remaining questions go unanswered?

What Questions Are Answered

Marx's question which has been answered most fully by militancy surveys is: Does support for militant means overlap with support for any particular political or economic ends? We know that black militants think ill of their local government and distrust American politicians and political institutions. We also know that black militants are particularly dissatisfied with their economic position and with their limited economic mobility. Yet among white militancy studies, we have difficulty uncovering comparable data or more than minimal answers to Marx's questions. Neither of the two major studies dealing with antiblack militancy tell us whether whites who feel politically powerless or politically distrustful are more militant. The limited comparable data do indicate, however, that antiblack militants feel dissatisfied with their mayor and with community services, and oppose black protests and federal aid to cities.

　　Black and white militancy surveys also provide a hint of an answer concerning the objective class base of militancy. Among blacks, the most militant tend to be the better educated. Among whites, the best educated and those with the best jobs are most willing militantly to oppose the government, while those with less education and worse jobs are generally more willing militantly to oppose blacks.

What Questions Remain

Unfortunately, we find more remaining questions than answered questions. Do militant, violent means fall on a continuum with nonmilitant, peaceful means? Paige, among others, attempts to answer this question in his study of Newark's black rioters. But studies dealing with whites provide no comprehensive answer. Although we know that politically active whites are more likely to support militant means to fight against governmental injustice, we do not really know the extent to which white support for violence overlaps with white support for less militant means.[28] Although we know that Los Angeles black militants feel that the outcome of the Watts riot was favorable (and hence that militant tactics are effective), we have no comparable answer for whites.[29] An important question thus remains: Are whites who perceive militant means as effective more likely to be antiblack and antigovernmental militants?

Most serious, however, are the lack of answers to three unsettling questions: Do black militancy and white militancy arise from the same sources? Do antiblack militancy among whites and antigovernmental militancy among whites result from similar motives? Do antiblack and antigovernmental militancy among whites reflect basic dissatisfaction with inequalities and inadequacies in the American socio-political structure? Until we provide at least tentative answers to at least some of these questions, we cannot claim to understand white political violence in today's and tomorrow's United States.

Why Do the Remaining Questions Go Unanswered

Why do the remaining questions go unanswered? The Marxist ideologue would assert that the questions go unanswered because social scientists surveying white militancy fail to study Marx and to employ a Marxian framework. But we cannot proffer such a facile or self-confident answer. We can only hazard a tentative guess: perhaps crucial questions remain unanswered because they were not thought of beforehand; and perhaps they were not thought of beforehand because too few students of militancy based their research designs upon a clearly delineated theory specifying the relationships among perceived political and social structural inadequacies, political ends, and political means.

Theoretical Inadequacies: Research designs on militancy were often constructed without the use of any underlying theory. This has led to theoretical and conceptual difficulties in interpreting findings. For example, the two major multi-city militancy surveys conducted under the auspices of the Kerner and Eisenhower Commissions contain a theoretical gaggle of independent variables: anomic authoritarianism, perceived discrimination, political vengeance, and assassination relief. Some independent variables are cross-tabulated with militancy measures, others are not. We are not presented with the theoretical reasoning which determined the choice of questions or the choice of particular items to be cross-tabulated. National commissions too often accepted the polling mentality, if not its methodology. The polling mentality most certainly has its advantages: studies flowing from commission data are individually excellent and produce many fascinating findings. Yet these studies have neither produced a cumulative body of comparable findings, nor contributed to refining or building a political theory of militancy.

Much survey literature on black militancy suffers from general theoretical inadequacies resulting from the absence of a shared theoretical framework.[30c] In some instances this has led to hit or miss interview schedules. Is the most obvious question always the best one? Sometimes yes, sometimes no. A large group of surveys on black militancy include perceived structural inadequacies as independent variables. But researchers operationalize perceived structural inadequacies in a multitude of ways, with a multitude of dissimilar emphases: political alienation, discrimination, consumer and employment discontent. The presence of theoretical frameworks in these studies would have encouraged scholars to ask: Is the most obvious question — alienation for example — the best indicator of perceived structural inadequacies? The use of a middle-level theoretical framework such as Marx's would have led to greater uniformity in independent variables, and greater uniformity in operationalizing perceived structural inadequacies. Greater uniformity would lead to greater comparability of survey results. And greater comparability of results would give us the opportunity to refine political science theory and finally begin seriously to build a truly cumulative political science.

The survey literature on white militancy has been blighted to an even greater extent by the lack of a shared theoretical framework.[d] If the absence of a theoretical framework in surveys of black militancy leads to difficulties in cumulating findings — a problem which is more immediately important to social scientists than to the general public — the lack of a theoretical framework in surveys dealing with white militancy has had potentially serious political consequences. Perceived structural inadequacies, a major focus of black militancy surveys, received short shrift by those studying white militancy. Investigators failed to ask a crucial question: Does white militancy derive from the same sources as black militancy? The possibilities of "white backlash" against inflation, unemployment, or unequal opportunity were given too little attention in reports touching on white militancy, although similar issues were fully explored in black militancy studies.

Conceptual Inadequacies: The absence of an underlying theoretical framework sometimes results in inadequate conceptualization of militancy. Researchers operationalize militancy in numerous ways, ranging from self-reported riot involvement, to approval of riots and other violent means, to self-projections of willingness to engage in militant activities. The difficulty lies not only in the

---

[c]Theoretical frameworks have been utilized. Ransford, *op. cit.,* based his research design upon a clearly delineated theoretical framework. Paige, *op. cit.,* Paige and Caplan, *op. cit.,* and Sears and McConahay, "Racial Socialization, Comparison Levels, and the Watts Riot," *op. cit.,* all do theoretically fascinating analyses. Murphy and Watson, *op. cit.,* also base their research upon a general theory of structural position, discontent, and militancy. Singer et al., *op. cit.,* employ Smelser's value-added approach. Yet these studies, individually excellent as they are, do not share a common theoretical framework, and are thus not truly cumulative.

[d]The excellent, recently published study by Blumenthal and her colleagues was based upon a clearly defined, heavily psychologically oriented, theoretical framework.

existence of a multitude of minimally comparable dependent variables, but also in the occasional failure to separate political ends from political means. Are the determinants of radical political ends the same as the determinants of militant political means? Can an individual hold radical ends while rejecting militant means for achieving those ends? Because of the two-dimensional nature of some militancy scales, some surveys cannot answer these questions.[31]

Several scholars employing single item militancy indicators fall prey to another conceptual shortcoming: they explore primarily the most militant political means, such as rioting, gun-toting, or counter-rioting. The last decade reveals that violence is not always synonymous with militancy; other political means also comprise militancy. Some scholars unintentionally foster the notion that rioting and violence are generically different from other political means. The existence of a continuum of political means, ranging from conventional, nonmilitant activities to unconventional, militant activities is assumed to be absent. Even those researchers who construct elegant militancy indexes have sometimes not fully explored conventional political activity and inactivity, thus biasing their research designs towards the assumption that political means do not lie on a continuum. What are the ramifications of this assumption? If political means are treated as if they are on a true continuum, then it is possible to determine the precise nature of the relationship between political means and political ends. Yet if respondents are queried principally about whether they would or would not use militant means to attain a particular end, then it is difficult to determine whether they would prefer to attain the same end through nonmilitant means. Many of our militancy indicators overdramatize and misrepresent support for violence among both blacks and whites.

A final conceptual difficulty is evident in all of the reviewed white militancy surveys, with the notable exception of those completed by Levy, and by Blumenthal and her colleagues. In each research design, militancy has been conceptualized and operationalized in terms of only a single target; researchers do not investigate antiblack militancy and antigovernmental militancy within the same research design. Researchers fail to broaden their dependent variable to include the possibility that respondents might endorse militant means to achieve some political ends, but reject militant means for achieving other ends. White militancy studies leave readers with an impression which empirical evidence only partially supports: the dissatisfactions lying behind antiblack militancy are totally different from the dissatisfactions lying behind antigovernmental militancy.

Conclusion

Imagine how different these surveys would have been if scholars had rigorously employed a middle-level theoretical framework! Researchers would have been forced to confront their own political and theoretical assumptions. Rather than inadvertently implying different causes for white and black militancy, for antigovernmental and antiblack militancy, survey researchers would have first determined if militancy arising from both racial groups and directed at both racial and governmental targets possesses similar origins. The same assumptions and questions would have been applied to both blacks and whites, to both those who advocate antiblack militancy and those who advocate antigovernmental militancy.

The use of a shared middle-level theoretical framework would have had additional advantages for militancy students. Rather than a multitude of noncomparable indicators of perceived structural inadequacies, scholars starting from similar theoretical vantage points would have employed indicators with at least theoretical comparability. Haphazard independent variables with no theoretical justifications would have been eliminated from research designs. Greater uniformity in defining and conceptualizing militancy would result from using a middle-level theory. Scholars would be wary of building multi-item militancy indexes which include some questions on political ends and other questions on political means, and many questions on unconventional, militant means but few questions on conventional, nonmilitant means. In short, political scientists would be able to cumulate findings and thus begin constructing and refining theories of white militancy.

3 Building a Theory of Militancy

Let us assume for the sake of argument that recent research had disproved once and for all every one of Marx's individual theses. Even if this were to be proved, every serious 'orthodox' Marxist would still be able to accept all such modern findings without reservation and hence dismiss all of Marx's theses in toto – without having to renounce his orthodoxy for a single moment. Orthodox Marxism, therefore, does not imply the uncritical acceptance of the results of Marx's investigations. It is not the 'belief' in this or that thesis, nor the exegesis of a 'sacred' book. On the contrary, orthodoxy refers exclusively to method.[1]

Georg Lukacs

Introduction

Survey research on black and white militancy has been flawed by the lack of a shared theoretical framework. Important questions about the relationship between socio-political dissatisfactions and white militancy remain unanswered; these questions, although partially addressed in the plethora of studies on black militancy, received less attention by those investigating white militancy. White militancy survey researchers fail to raise or to answer many of Marx's questions.

But perhaps Marx's questions are not the right ones. Incisive as his questions are, perhaps they provide only an incomplete theoretical framework for investigating today's white militancy; perhaps social scientists have done well by ignoring Marx's questions.

Since Richard Centers' 1949 study on *The Psychology of Social Classes,* American social scientists have devoted substantial attention to answering one of Marx's questions: What is the relationship between class consciousness and political attitudes?[2] Despite widely differing operational and theoretical definitions of class consciousness, surveys have largely confirmed Marx's hypothesizing: class conscious Americans tend to hold more liberal political views and to act as a more cohesive political group than other Americans.[3] Yet these surveys, with their heavy emphasis on political ends, offer us little direct assistance in understanding the use of militant means. Further, these studies have been generally based upon a Marxian framework uncorrected for inadequacies in Marx's own writings.

The Limitations of Marx's Perspective

Marx's questions, both as he posed them himself and as they have been posed by survey researchers dealing with class consciousness, can be usefully adapted into a theoretical framework for investigating white militancy. But Marx's questions cannot stand as they are; conceptual weaknesses in Marx's approach must first be remedied. These conceptual weaknesses lie in two elements of his thoughts which are integral to building a theoretical framework concerning white militancy: first, Marx's concept of relative dissatisfactions and subjective class consciousness; and second, Marx's concept of the relationship between dissatisfactions and revolutionary political action.

Relative Dissatisfactions and Subjective Class Consciousness

Marx's theorizing contains an overly restricted view of relative dissatisfactions and subjective class consciousness. In its simplest form, the Marxian viewpoint is that the productive workers' awareness of the relative economic gap between themselves and the unproductive middle class will lead to disaffection with the objective class structure. This simple Marxian formulation implies that radical criticisms of both the government and the objective class structure stem solely from economic dissatisfactions. Noneconomic dissatisfactions contribute nothing to the growth of subjective class consciousness and radicalism. The white worker may be dissatisfied with his life and with the American socio-political structure in which he lives; yet if he is not unhappy with his economic lot, he can never be a radical or attain subjective class consciousness.

Such a formulation only partially represents Marx's actual theorizing. As was pointed out in Chapter 1, Marx defines subjective class consciousness as awareness of both the nature of the objective class structure and the individual's position in the objective class structure relative to other classes. In illustrating the nature of these relative differences and the dissatisfactions which flow from these differences, Marx occasionally cites examples of subjective class consciousness stemming from noneconomic grievances.

In a famous 1849 passage, for example, Marx points to the dissatisfactions engendered by the worker's comparison of his adequate yet small house with the neighboring palace. The comparison of the two buildings leads the worker to think of his own house as a hut. According to Marx, the worker will then realize that he "has no social position at all to maintain, or but a very insignificant one," and he "will always find himself more uncomfortable, more dissatisfied, more cramped within his four walls."[4] Marx here does not discuss subjective class consciousness in terms of such purely economic factors as the person's perception of differences between himself and others along the dimensions of ownership/nonownership of the means of production, control/lack of control over the products of one's work, or productive/unproductive labor. Rather,

Marx speaks of subjective class consciousness primarily as the person's perception of his own relative lack of status and goods.

Marx never adequately develops this point. He supplies only hints about the noneconomic dimensions of subjective class consciousness and the noneconomic determinants of political ends. It was left to Max Weber to supplement Marx's theorizing.

Writing in the early twentieth century, Weber broadened Marx's concept of subjective class consciousness and identified its individual dimensions. Weber points to the distribution of power as the fundamental determinant of relative dissatisfactions and political ends. He defines power as ". . . the chance of a man or of a number of men to realize their own will in a communal action even against the resistance of others who are participating in the action."[5] Marx would have readily agreed with Weber's definition; but Marx would have added the caveats that all power is economically determined, and that all dissatisfactions with one's power are basically economic dissatisfactions. For Marx, "power" is largely synonymous with "economic power." Identifying a major conceptual limitation of Marx's restrictive definition of power, Weber points out that:

'Economically conditioned' power is not, of course, identical with 'power' as such. On the contrary, the emergence of economic power may be the consequence of power existing on other grounds. Man does not strive for power only in order to enrich himself economically. Power, including economic power, may be valued 'for its own sake.' Very frequently the striving for power is also conditioned by the social 'honor' it entails. Not all power, however, entails social honor: The typical American Boss, as well as the typical big speculator, deliberately relinquishes social honor. Quite generally, 'mere economic' power, and especially 'naked' money power, is by no means a recognized basis of social honor. Nor is power the only basis of social honor. Indeed, social honor, or prestige, may even be the basis of political or economic power, and very frequently has been.[6]

Weber thus dissects Marx's construct into three component parts: social status, economic class, and political power.

According to Weber, status is ". . . every typical component of the life fate of men that is determined by a specific, positive or negative, social estimation of *honor*."[7] Individuals with common status situations constitute status groups. Status groups bear little resemblance to Marx's objective class groupings. Unlike objective class groupings,

[1. Status groups are] often of an amorphous kind. . . . Both propertied and propertyless people can belong to the same status group, and frequently they do with very tangible consequences.[8]
[2.] . . . the place of 'status groups' is within the social order, that is, within the sphere of the distribution of 'honor.'[9]

The second dimension of power — class — lies solely within the economic order. The individual's class situation is his "... typical chance for a supply of goods, external living conditions, and personal life experiences, in so far as this chance is determined by the amount and kind of power, or lack of such, to dispose of goods or skills for the sake of income in a given economic order."[10]

Weber's definition of class parallels Marx's definition of objective class. Like Marx's objective classes, Weber's classes are "stratified according to their relations to the production and acquisition of goods."[11] And again like Marx, Weber maintains that a person's class situation is largely determined by his property or lack of property.[12] Weber, however, goes beyond Marx and refers to three additional bases of class relations and differences between classes: creditor-debtor differences; differences between wage-earners and those who pay wages; and differences between the sellers and the consumers of goods.[13]

The least well defined of Weber's three dimensions is political party. In Weber's words, parties are "... oriented toward the acquisition of social 'power,' that is to say, toward influencing a communal action no matter what its content may be."[14] While both classes and status groups are objective structural groupings, a party exists only in so far as its members consciously cooperate in their pursuit of common ends: "for party actions are always directed toward a goal which is striven for in planned manner."[15] Weber implies that while everyone holds positions along the status and class dimensions, only some hold a position along the party dimension. If Weber had attempted to make the party dimension more congruent with the status and class dimensions, he might have redefined the individual's party situation as his typical chance for control or influence over governmental and/or communal action and decision-making. In keeping with this redefinition, a party group could then be defined as a number of people, all of whom share approximately equal chances for control or influence over governmental and/or communal action and decision-making.

Weber neither equates the individual's objective placement on these three dimensions with his subjective placement, nor believes that a direct relationship exists between objective placement and political attitudes. Weber maintains that only after the individual becomes aware of his class or status situations could they directly influence his ends:[16]

For however different life chances may be, this fact in itself, according to all experience, by no means gives birth to 'class action' (communal action by the members of a class). The fact of being conditioned and the results of the class situation must be distinctly recognizable.[17]

Cognition of the status or class situation precedes dissatisfaction with the situation, and dissatisfactions precede action to remedy the situation.

Weber's discussion of the three stratification dimensions has frequently been interpreted as a refutation of Marx. Weber, however, intended to elaborate and expand upon Marx's theorizing, not to refute him; as Irving Zeitlin points out regarding C. Wright Mills' view, "Weber ... was perhaps the greatest revisionist of Marx."[18] In keeping with Marx, class is important in Weber's three dimensional schema. Weber's status and political party dimensions could be viewed as elaborations of Marx's concept of objective class.

Any divergence between Marx and Weber does not derive from their differing definitions of status or class, or from their disagreement over the number of stratification dimensions. Rather, the divergence arises from Weber's and Marx's differing assumptions about whether economic class, social status, and political power are both conceptually and empirically distinct. Marx never explicitly distinguishes economic class from social status, or either from political power, because he believes that all three dimensions totally overlap: the individual's class situation determines both his status situation and his party situation. Weber, on the other hand, asserts that while overlap frequently occurs, it is not inevitable: individuals with the same status situation may be in different classes, and individuals in different classes may be in the same party or status group. Since overlap is not inevitable, the three dimensions should remain conceptually distinct.

Weber's "Class, Status, Party" leads to a threefold revision of Marx's theorizing on subjective class consciousness. First, we must revise Marx's concept of relative dissatisfactions. Marx assumes that relative dissatisfactions are generated by perceived economic inequalities. Weber's scheme suggests that relative dissatisfactions can also flow from perceived political and status inequalities. Dissatisfactions can occur along any or all of the three dimensions; an individual can be dissatisfied with his economic standing, but not with his social status or political power.

Second, Marx's concept of radicalism must be revised. Marx believes that subjectively conscious workers will hold radical ends. Marx defines radicalism as consisting of both political and economic attitudes; his criteria for revolutionary political action are based on the assumption that radical political ends and radical economic ends coincide. Yet Weber's logic suggests that if the individual can be dissatisfied with his political position while at the same time be satisfied with his economic position, then he can also hold radical political ends without holding radical economic ends. The coincidence of radical political ends with radical economic ends should be tested, not assumed.

Third, Weber's expansion of Marx implies that Marx's theorizing on the development of subjective class consciousness needs revision. Marx recognized that noneconomic factors could impede the growth of subjective class consciousness within the objective working class. In discussing the United States, England, and Germany, Marx asserted that the presence of ethnic divisions within the working class hindered the development of subjective class consciousness.[19] But Marx did not recognize, as Weber did, the possibility of other nonoverlapping cleavages within the objective working class. Similarly, Marx did not realize, as Weber's scheme implicitly suggests, that internal working class cleavages could conceivably result in a portion of the workers rationally holding political or status interests closer to the middle class than to other workers.

Subjective Class Consciousness and Political Action

Despite the importance of political action in Marx's theorizing, his writings on this subject are often ambiguous and confusing. Part of this confusion results from Marx's frequent failure to distinguish class consciousness from revolutionary political action. As Paulo Freire indicates in his *Pedagogy of the Oppressed:*

In order for the oppressed to be able to wage the struggle for their liberation, they must perceive the reality of oppression not as a closed world from which there is no exit, but as a limiting situation which they can transform. *This perception is a necessary but not a sufficient condition for liberation; it must become the motivating force for liberating action.* [italics added] [20]

Marx assumes that knowledge of a relative gap between oneself and those at the top of the objective class structure, dissatisfaction with that gap, and action to lessen the gap are highly correlated with each other. Marx often defines subjective class consciousness in terms of both political attitudes and political action. Marx implies that dissatisfied individuals will automatically take action to relieve their dissatisfactions.

Marx combines conceptually distinct elements. He fails to acknowledge that the worker could be aware of his own relative standing in the objective class structure, and not be dissatisfied with his standing. He fails to perceive that the worker could be dissatisfied with his class standing, yet be unwilling to take action to alter the objective class structure.

If both Karl Marx and Max Weber were living today, they would ask different but complementary research questions about white militancy. Where Marx would search for the sources of militancy and radicalism in white workers' economic dissatisfactions with their relative standing in the objective class structure, Weber would point to status, economic, and political discontents. Writing today, Marx would assert that economic discontents are all-important to America's white working and middle classes, that status and political power discontents among whites derive from their more basic economic discontents, and that radicalism principally springs from economic discontents. Weber, on the other hand, would stress that economic, political, and status dissatisfactions do not necessarily overlap, and that these three different types of dissatisfactions could lead to three different types of radicalism among whites.

In explaining white radicalism and militancy, Marx would maintain that the person who knows of his own disadvantaged position will become dissatisfied, that this will lead to radicalism, and that radicalism inevitably will result in political action to achieve radical ends. If the radical regards unconventional, violent political means as effective, he will also become a militant. Weber, however, would quickly challenge Marx's statements concerning the relationships among discontent, radicalism, and action. Weber would see no sure links between knowledge and dissatisfactions, or between dissatisfactions and action.

The urban white worker who recognizes his relatively disadvantaged position might not become dissatisfied; if he does become dissatisfied, he nevertheless might not take action to remedy his dissatisfactions.

Building a Theoretical Perspective on Militancy

Marx's and Weber's questions have been partially answered in survey research; many hypotheses derived from their theorizing are neither novel nor unique. Why then resurrect their theories once again? Through paying close attention to their theorizing, we can derive explicit definitions of conceptually distinct variables. Relying on Marx's and Weber's theorizing will also encourage raising theoretically important questions about white militancy. Finally, using Marx and Weber as our theoretical backdrop will help us to answer major questions which have not been fully addressed in militancy research: Do white and black militancy derive from the same sources? Does white militancy result from basic dissatisfactions with inequalities in the American socio-political structure?

Defining the Variables — Independent Variables

Discussed in detail here are the power dimensions and their respective levels. With reference to Marx and Weber we will deal with social, political and economic power.

Power Dimensions. Following Weber's revision of Marx, we will assume that societal power is hierarchically stratified along three dimensions: social status, political power, and economic power. Status is the amount of prestige or respect accorded to an individual or group by others in society. Status, as Weber implies, contains numerous internal hierarchies, such as race and ethnicity. These internal hierarchies are conceptually distinct, and may or may not empirically overlap. Here we shall deal solely with the overall respect dimension.

Political power will be defined as the individual's typical opportunity for influence over governmental decision-making. Like status, political power represents a general stratification dimension, and contains numerous internal hierarchies. These internal hierarchies are specific to both governmental level and individual issues. The person's opportunity for influence varies from issue to issue, and from governmental level to governmental level; he may have great opportunity for influence over school-bussing decisions at the local governmental level, and little opportunity for influence over foreign policy decisions at the national governmental level. Here we will focus on an issue-specific dimension at the local governmental level, and on the overall political power dimension.

Arriving at an adequate definition of economic power presents a more complex problem. Are we to adopt Marx's tripartite definition, consisting of productive/unproductive labor, control/lack of control over the products of one's labor, and ownership/nonownership of the means of production? Or should we employ Weber's even more complex definition, based on property and lack of property but consisting of three other internal hierarchies as well?

Keeping in mind Kornhauser's warning that "nothing useful is gained by pretending that a particular chosen simplification of class is the true account. . . .," we will combine elements of both Marx's and Weber's definitions.[21] Economic power will be conceptualized as one basic dimension with three subsidiary hierarchies. The basic dimension is whether the individual performs productive or unproductive labor; in Marx's words, the productive worker is one who ". . . reproduces capital [and not just] . . . exchanges his labour for income."[22] One possible indicator for productive/unproductive labor is the individual's occupation. In addition to the basic productive/unproductive labor dimension, there are three additional internal hierarchies of economic power: in Weber's terms, these are labor power (employment/unemployment, and wage earner/wage payer), credit power, and consumption power. The three hierarchies are conceptually distinct, and empirically they may or may not overlap. The data to be discussed in the following chapters deal with the labor power hierarchy.

Levels of Power Dimensions. Each stratification dimension exists on three levels: the objective level, the subjective cognitive level, and the subjective affective level.[23] The objective level corresponds to the individual's position in the particular power dimension as determined by either a series of structural characteristics, such as income, occupation, and so forth, or by typical judgments of others in society. Whether structural characteristics or typical judgments are operationally used to place individuals in the objective levels depends largely upon pragmatic considerations. Structural characteristics, such as income, are typically assumed to be adequate measures of the individual's placement in the objective economic class dimension; on the other hand, typical judgments are generally used to determine the individual's placement in the objective status dimension.[24]

The subjective cognitive level refers to the individual's own conception of his position in each of the three hierarchies. As Marx points out, the key variable at the subjective cognitive level is the extent to which the individual perceives a gap between himself, and others who he identifies as similar to himself, and those who he perceives as at the top of the particular power hierarchy. The subjective cognitive level is similar to W.G. Runciman's concept of the magnitude of relative deprivation.[25]

The subjective affective level corresponds to the extent to which a person is dissatisfied with the gap which he perceives between himself, and others like himself, and those who he perceives of as at the top of the particular power hierarchy. The subjective affective level is similar to Runciman's definition of "the degree of a relative deprivation . . . [as] the intensity with which it is felt."[26]

The objective level, the subjective cognitive level, and the subjective affective level are conceptually distinct and conceptually independent. As Marx and Weber repeatedly assert, a person may objectively possess little economic power (low position on the objective level of the economic power dimension) and nevertheless may perceive himself as the possessor of great economic power (high position on the subjective cognitive level of the economic power dimension). From political conventional wisdom about white militancy we can draw another example: the white worker who objectively possesses average opportunity for influence over city decisions on bussing his children to school (medium position on the objective level of the bussing issue, local governmental internal hierarchy of the political power dimension), but who perceives himself as possessing no opportunity for influence as compared to blacks (low position on the subjective cognitive level of the bussing issue, local governmental internal hierarchy). The subjective affective level is similarly conceptually distinct from both the objective level and the subjective cognitive level. A person could be objectively politically powerless (low position on the objective level of the political power dimension), perceive himself as politically powerless (low position on the subjective cognitive level of the political power dimension), and yet not be dissatisfied with his lack of political power (high position on the subjective affective level of the political power dimension).

The conceptual independence of the three dimensions should not be confused with their empirical independence. Weber believes that the dimensions empirically overlap, although he does not see the complete overlap envisioned by Marx. An urban white with high objective status and substantial objective economic power is likely to possess substantial objective political power as well. However, overlap of the three dimensions at each level cannot be assumed, and must be specifically tested.

Even greater empirical overlap probably exists among the three levels within each dimension. An individual who is objectively economically powerless is more likely to perceive himself as powerless than as powerful. An individual who thinks of himself as politically powerless is likely to be dissatisfied with his position. Marx frequently focuses on the cases in which congruence between the objective and subjective cognitive levels does not exist: those people who are objectively powerless, but do not recognize their disadvantaged position. Weber similarly points to the importance of linkages between the levels. Thus, we must not assume empirical overlap between objective powerlessness, subjective cognitive powerlessness, and subjective affective powerlessness.

Intervening Variables

Governmental Acquiescence. Marx implies that the choice of any particular means to achieve a specific end will be determined by the individual's perception of the likelihood of that means accomplishing the end. Sorel, Gurr, and Gamson make similar assertions. In *Reflections on Violence,* Sorel maintains that "humanitarian" regimes will be more likely than totalitarian regimes to stimulate violent protest tactics.[27] "Humanitarian" regimes rapidly accede to the demands of violent protestors; other citizens, seeing the success of violent means, will then employ those means to achieve their own ends. Gurr, in his *Why Men Rebel,* speaks of utilitarian justifications for violence: "the greater they believe the potential gains to be, the more justifiable violence is likely to appear to them."[28] The more utilitarian justifications an individual can garner for the use of violent means, then the more likely he is to employ those means. In *Power and Discontent,* Gamson notes that the successful use of a particular means is likely to promote further use of similar means.[29]

In this work, actual governmental acquiescence refers to whether the use of a particular means against the government by a group succeeds in achieving the desired end. Perceived governmental acquiescence will be the extent to which a person believes that the use of a particular means against the government has been or is likely to be successful in achieving an end desired by some group. Actual governmental acquiescence and perceived governmental acquiescence are conceptually distinct and are often empirically unrelated; the use of riots as a political means by blacks may have failed to achieve the desired end, but many whites probably perceive that local and national governments acquiesced to the use of violent means by blacks.

Myth. In his discussions of factors which facilitate the growth of subjective class consciousness, Marx stresses the importance of horizontal communication within the working class. Marx implies that a person's choice of both means and ends will be affected by his familiarity with others who share his dissatisfactions, and who help him to recognize the ways in which those dissatisfactions can be relieved. Other authors make similar assertions. Weber points out that "the fact of being conditioned and the results of the class situation must be distinctly recognizable;"[30] the existence of horizontal communication aids the worker in recognizing both "the fact of being conditioned" and "the results of the class situation."

Sorel and Gurr develop similar hypotheses, but base these hypotheses on slightly different factors. Sorel maintains that before a group engages in violence, it first must be permeated by a "myth:"

In the course of this study one thing has always been present in my mind, which seemed to me so evident that I did not think it worthwhile to lay much stress on it — that men who are participating in a great social movement always picture their coming action as a battle in which their cause is certain to triumph. These constructions . . . I propose to call myths. . . . [31]

Gurr writes of the importance of doctrines which provide justifications for political violence: "the relative effectiveness of such doctrines varies with the extent to which they provide rationales for men to act on their discontent. . . ."[32]

Myth will here be defined as groups, individuals, or ideologies which identify dissatisfactions, and propose the proper means and/or ends for relieving those dissatisfactions. Myth could thus include an ideology, union, or candidate for public office. The extent of the individual's familiarity with such myths represents an intervening variable between powerlessness and his choice of means and ends.

Dependent Variables

Power Ends. An individual's ends are the desired changes he would like to see in a particular power dimension, the desired distribution of power in that dimension, the desired condition of the dimension, or the approval or disapproval of an action taken to alter that dimension. For example, political ends could include desire for more white political power over bussing, desire for less political power wielded by blacks on bussing decisions, support for a candidate opposing bussing, and desire that the government not employ bussing to achieve school integration. Marx asserts that a person's choice of ends tells us nothing about his choice of means; a white worker may desire a massive increase of his political power over city government bussing decisions, but may choose totally pacific methods for achieving that increase.

Ends are specific to each of the three power dimensions, and to the various internal hierarchies within each dimension. Status ends are distinct from political ends, and both are distinct from economic ends. The conceptual distinctiveness of ends implies that an individual can desire a massive redistribution of power in the political dimension, without desiring any redistribution of power in the economic dimension. Illustrative of this would be the middle class white who is satisfied with his economic standing, but wants more influence over local governmental decisions on school desegregation.

Most ends are continuous variables: an individual desires more or less power redistribution, or he desires a more conservative or a more liberal government. However, one particular type of political ends – support or opposition to a candidate – could be conceptualized as either a dichotomous or a continuous variable. Ends lying at either extreme of a particular continuum will be referred to as radical ends.

Power Means. Power means are the methods which an individual utilizes to achieve an end. The available means differ from dimension to dimension. Voting is a means for redistributing political power, but it is not necessarily a means for changing the status dimension.

All means, regardless of which dimension they are being applied to, are continuous variables. A person may choose to riot or not to riot, or to vote or to abstain from voting. However, we should avoid conceptualizing political means as rioting or not rioting. Rather, we should think in terms of a choice between rioting and other possible acts; the individual may choose to vote instead of rioting. The range of means extends from pacific to violent activities; means lying at the more violent, less institutionalized end of the continuum, such as rioting and mass protesting, will be referred to as militant means. The person's choice of means tells us nothing about the political ends he hopes to achieve; he may choose militant means to accomplish moderate ends.

Relationships Among the Variables: The Sources of Radicalism and Militancy

The Sources of Radicalism

Basic to both the Marxian and Weberian frameworks is the assertion that powerlessness leads to radicalism. However, Marx and Weber would differ in their conceptions of the precise link between powerlessness and radicalism, and in their conceptions of the nature of the radicalism produced by powerlessness.

For Marx and Weber objective powerlessness is not a sufficient condition for the growth of radicalism. Marx fails adequately to distinguish subjective cognitive powerlessness from subjective affective powerlessness; he implies that the objectively powerless individual who is also either cognitively or affectively powerless will eventually hold radical ends. Weber implicitly distinguishes among objective powerlessness, subjective cognitive powerlessness, and subjective affective powerlessness. Radicalism would flow from subjective affective powerlessness, and not from objective powerlessness or subjective cognitive powerlessness by themselves.

Marx implicitly defines radicalism in terms of the person's desire to redistribute power. Marx, however, equates the desire for power redistribution with the desire for power equalization in the political and economic dimensions. Economic powerlessness would stimulate the individual's desire for both economic and political power equalization.

Implied by Weber's framework is a different definition of radicalism. A Weberian definition of radicalism would be the desire for a total redistribution of power; the desired redistribution could result in drastic inequalities. The Weberian definition does not confine radicalism to any single dimension. Marx defines radicalism in terms of a primary source and a primary dimension, but Weber would define three radicalisms flowing from the three different sources of economic, political, and status powerlessness. Where Marx defines radicalism in terms of egalitarian redistribution and focuses on one extreme of the ends continuum, Weber would probably focus on radicalism as redistribution, which can be either egalitarian (left) or drastically inegalitarian (right).

The Sources of Militancy

Marx assumes that means lie on a continuum from conventional, nonmilitant tactics to unconventional, militant tactics, and that the subjectively conscious worker will inevitably act to relieve his dissatisfactions. The willingness to take action is thus an integral part of Marx's definition of subjective class consciousness. Marx, however, does not define the content of the action which will be taken by the subjectively conscious worker.

The sources of militancy do not lie in a person's political views: the radical, subjectively conscious worker is no more likely to employ militant means to achieve his ends than the moderate worker. The white worker who opposes school bussing is no more likely to use violence than the white worker who favors school bussing.

Means are conceptually independent of ends. The individual's choice of militant or nonmilitant means will be determined not by whether he holds rightist or leftist ends, but by his perception of governmental acquiescence. The greater the extent to which a person believes that the use of a particular means against the government has been or is likely to be successful in achieving the desired end, then the more likely he will be to employ that tactic to achieve his own ends. A white who thinks that the government has acquiesced to black use of militant means during riots – whether or not he agrees with the ends supported by the black rioters – will be likely to support militant means in achieving his own ends.

Common Sources of Radicalism and Militancy

Marx and Weber imply that objective powerlessness is not automatically transposed into either radical ends or a particular means to achieve those ends. A mediating factor exists between dissatisfactions, on the one hand, and the choice of ends and means, on the other hand. This mediating factor is the individual's familiarity with myths – groups, individuals, or ideologies which identify dissatisfactions and propose proper means and ends for relieving those dissatisfactions.

The powerless individual who is familiar with a myth that both identifies his dissatisfactions and identifies the radical end of redistributing power will be more likely to hold radical ends than the powerless individual who is unfamiliar with such a myth. The powerless individual who is familiar with a myth that identifies his dissatisfactions and suggests militant means for relieving those dissatisfactions will be more likely to employ militant means than the powerless individual who is unfamiliar with such a myth. The Newark white who is subjectively affectively politically powerless on school bussing and knows of Tony Imperiale is more likely to endorse militant means than the similarly powerless Newark white who is unfamiliar with Tony Imperiale.

I spoke of this piece of work we were doing as 'curious.' I had better amplify this.

It seems to me curious, not to say obscene and thoroughly terrifying, that it could occur to an association of human beings drawn together through need and chance and for profit into a company, an organ of journalism, to pry intimately into the lives of an undefended and appallingly damaged group of human beings, an ignorant and helpless rural family, for the purpose of parading the nakedness, disadvantage and humiliation of these lives before another group of human beings, in the name of science, of 'honest journalism' (whatever that paradox may mean), of humanity, of social fearlessness, for money, and for a reputation for crusading and for unbias which, when skillfully enough qualified, is exchangeable at any bank for money (and in politics, for votes, job patronage, abelincolnism, etc.); and that these people could be capable of meditating this prospect without the slightest doubt of their qualification to do an 'honest' piece of work, and with a conscience better than clear, and in the virtual certitude of almost unanimous public approval. It seems curious, further, that the assignment of this work should have fallen to persons having so extremely different a form of respect for the subject, and responsibility toward it, that from the first and inevitably they counted their employers, and that Government likewise to which one of them was bonded, among their most dangerous enemies, acted as spies, guardians, and cheats, and trusted no judgment, however authoritative it claimed to be, save their own: which in many aspects of the task before them was untrained and uninformed. It seems further curious that realizing the extreme corruptness and difficulty of the circumstances, and the unlikelihood of achieving in any untainted form what they wished to achieve, they accepted the work in the first place. And it seems curious still further that, with all their suspicion of and contempt for every person and thing to do with the situation, save only for the tenants and for themselves, and their own intentions, and with all their realization of the seriousness and mystery of the subject, and of the human responsibility they undertook, they so little questioned or doubted their own qualifications for this work.

All of this, I repeat, seems to me curious, obscene, terrifying, and unfathomably mysterious. [1]

James Agee and Walker Evans

Introduction

The results of a survey we conducted in 1970 Boston provide an opportunity to explore several hypothetical relationships set forth in the preceding chapter.[2] Three hundred and one Boston white men holding blue- and white-collar jobs were interviewed; they were principally questioned about their reactions to school bussing and black riots. The political setting in which the survey was conducted and the operationalization of the variables will be described in this chapter.

Political Setting

Black Demands and White Reactions

Almost any large northern city could provide multiple examples of white reactions to black demands. Yet some cities better exemplify the complexities of the current racial situation than do others; Boston represents a particularly good site for investigating white militancy and white reactions to black demands. Inherent in Boston politics are all the intricacies of black-white relations in particular, and northern urban American politics in general.[3] Three issues which have largely dominated Boston politics in recent years serve to illustrate this complexity: the Racial Imbalance Act, the Roxbury rioting, and the political activities of Boston School Committeewoman, City Councilwoman, and U.S. Congresswoman Louise Day Hicks.

Racial Imbalance Act[4]

In the late years of the Johnson Administration and the early years of the Nixon administration, the Department of Health, Education and Welfare promoted school bussing as one means for increasing racial integration in the nation's public schools. HEW officials initially concentrated their attention upon southern states, and white resistance to bussing was therefore most prominent in the South. Yet 1971 efforts to achieve integration through bussing in Pontiac, Michigan, demonstrated that white resistance knows no geographical bounds, and that some northern whites, like some southern whites, are willing to employ violent means to oppose forced bussing. The Supreme Court's support for bussing as an acceptable tool for increasing school integration and President Nixon's opposition to bussing further confused many already disgruntled whites; those who favor school bussing find themselves adhering to national policy as set forth by the Supreme Court, while those who resist school bussing see themselves following national policy as established by the President.

The Boston school bussing controversy is especially noteworthy, for it began well before the brouhahas of other northern cities, and it was generated by home-state politicians, rather than by federal intervention. In 1963 and 1965, blacks protested de facto segregation in Boston schools by picketing the Boston School Committe, the nonpartisan, biennially elected group of six officials who control Boston's public schools. Although the School Committee displayed little interest in meeting the desegregation demands of Boston's black community, the Massachusetts state legislature did take action. In 1965, the Massachusetts Racial Imbalance Act was passed by the state legislature and approved by Governor Volpe. The law requires racial balancing of any public school in which more than 50% of the student body is nonwhite. State funds were to be withheld from any school district which did not submit an acceptable plan for racial balancing, and which did not show evidence of rapidly acting on their plan. A 1965 State Board of Education report recommended that bussing of both blacks and whites be used to achieve integration.

The Massachusetts Racial Imbalance Act was heralded by the U.S. Commission on Civil Rights, which suggested that the law, with its harsh financial penalty for noncompliance, should become the national model for state school desegregation laws. Yet those elected to the Boston School Committee in 1965 opposed the law. Committee members Hicks and O'Connor vehemently criticized the law as directed by the state legislature against Boston, as representing excessive state intervention into local politics, and as the vehicle through which the state government would do away with Boston's neighborhood schools. O'Connor's and Hicks' charges did contain elements of truth. Although the provisions of the Racial Imbalance Act apply equally to all Massachusetts school districts, it held considerably greater implications for Boston than for any other Massachusetts city. In fact, only three other Massachusetts cities were directly affected by the new law.

The Boston School Committee has been unable and unwilling to meet the desegregation requirements set forth in the Racial Imbalance Act. The State Attorney General's office has characterized "the city's battling record on racial imbalance ... [as] highly unsatisfactory."[5] According to State Board of Education estimates, the number of racially imbalanced schools in Boston has increased from forty-six in 1965 to sixty-five in 1971. At times, the School Committee has actively resisted complying with the law. In 1966, the Committee brought a suit challenging the constitutionality of the Racial Imbalance Act. When the suit reached the Massachusetts Supreme Judicial Court in 1967, the School Committee's arguments were rejected. In 1966-67, 6.3 million dollars in state education funds were temporarily withheld from Boston because of noncompliance with the law; several balancing plans had been submitted to the State Education Department and rejected as inadequate. Under this heavy financial pressure, the School Committee yielded to state demands; the approved balancing plan specified that two of Boston's imbalanced schools were to be closed, and that the children from these schools were to be bussed to less crowded, mostly white schools. State funding was restored. Since 1967, state education funds have been withheld from Boston several other times, culminating in the temporary withholding of fifty-two million dollars in 1972. In 1971 and 1972, the U.S. Department of Health, Education and Welfare threatened to withhold federal education funds because of the existence of "... two separate, racially identifiable school subsystems – one predominantly white and the other predominantly non-white" within Boston's public schools.[6] According to state spokesmen, the State Board of Education is now less interested in desegregation plans than in concrete evidence of "reasonable progress" toward desegregation. Rather than reasonable progress, the racial imbalance in Boston schools "is increasing each year at a dramatic rate."[7]

Roxbury Rioting[8]

Compared to the numerous deaths and massive property damage of such riots as Watts, Harlem, and Hough, the Boston disturbances of 1967 and 1968 were mild. No blacks died from police bullets, and neither the National Guard nor the army was employed to restore order. The 1967 riot was so mild that the National Commission on Civil Disorders did not classify it as a major disturbance. Although the disturbances were not nearly as bloody as those in other big cities, they nevertheless profoundly affected Boston politics.

The 1967 riot, which began during the late afternoon of June second, had an explicitly political content and genesis. The triggering incident behind the riot was a Mothers for Adequate Welfare (MAW) sit-in held at the Grove Hall Welfare Center in Roxbury. MAW protestors padlocked the Center's doors from the inside, and refused to allow police entrance into the building. Police, foreceably trying to gain entrance, were pelted with stones, bottles, and debris. The riot had started, and it was to continue for the next three nights.

Two themes were clearly articulated during the riot. First, welfare benefits were inadequate and welfare procedures unsatisfactory. Journalists, white politicians, and the black community all agreed that the MAW protests helped to spark the riot. During the meetings with Roxbury community leaders preceding the riot's end, the MAW's list of demands was discussed. Immediately after the riot, a biracial committee was established to investigate Boston's welfare system, and negotiations were conducted with MAW representatives.

The second theme, as in other 1960's black riots, was police behavior. Roxbury blacks accused police of using excessive force in ousting MAW protestors from the Grove Hall Welfare Center. Black youths, interviewed by reporters during the riot, constantly returned to the theme of police brutality:

Did you see what those cops did up there at the center? You seen them beat women like that? Well, we're going to get them now. They're as scared as we are.[9]

'That wasn't an attack on them [the police],' one of the teenagers said. 'We were defending ourselves. They are the ones who attacked us.'[10]

Reverend James Breedon, the widely respected director of the Commission on Church and Race of the Massachusetts Council of Churches, maintained that the police rioted, not the black people of Roxbury.

The 1968 disturbances, while less severe and less prolonged than the 1967 riot, served to remind Boston whites that black mass violence had become a part of their city's political process. Following the Martin Luther King assassination in April of 1968, several nights of sporadic stone-throwing at cars and fire-bombing occurred in Roxbury. Lieutenant Governor Francis W. Sargent placed the Massachusetts National Guard on standby alert, but never mobilized them. Three months later, fighting broke out after a city-sponsored soul concert, and a troublesome July night of window-smashing followed. In late September, further disturbances occurred as black youths engaged in two days of rock-throwing, stoning cars, and occasional clashes with police. As in 1967, the immediate cause of the disturbance was explicitly political. Black youths, demanding better school facilities, better teachers, a black student union, and a removal of a ban on the wearing of African attire, had been boycotting public schools. Blacks, frustrated by School Committee intransigence, were attempting to coerce the School Committee into accepting their demands and considering community control proposals. Black city councilman Thomas Atkins maintained that:

The dispute went into the streets because the school system was too rigid to respond. . . . What the kids are saying is, 'We took a look at ourselves and liked what we saw. And we're going to be ourselves in the streets, in our churches, and in the schools.'[11]

Louise Day Hicks

Louise Day Hicks, the lawyer daughter of beloved Boston Judge William S. Day, represents many of the contradictions of Boston politics; her political philosophy reflects both the liberalism and the conservatism of many American working class white ethnics. Recent Boston politics, and particularly white reactions to the Racial Imbalance Act and the 1967 and 1968 disturbances, cannot be explained without discussing Hicks' career.

Louise Day Hicks campaigns through skillfully appealing to the lower middle class and working class Italian and Irish areas of South Boston, Dorchester, East Boston, and Charlestown.[12] Thomas F. Pettigrew, in his artful empirical portrait of Hicks' supporters, points out that ". . . the pro-Hicks group resemble their Southern counterparts: these resisters of racial change were, as a group, less educated, poorer, and older than others in the sample."[13] But contrary to the impression commonly held by many non-Bostonians, Hicks has not based her political career solely on appealing to white bigotry. In her successful first campaign for a seat on the Boston School Committee, waged in 1961, she ran as a reform candidate, promising to remove politics from the administration of Boston's public schools. In her unsuccessful 1967 and 1971 campaigns for Boston's nonpartisan mayoralty, she continually pledged to remove "politics" from city administration. Hicks repeatedly pointed to her campaign's total dependence on small contributions and the refusal of any Boston politicians to support her: "I have no endorsements from any politicians. My campaign is a campaign of the people."[14]

Yet Louise Day Hicks' reformism is not the reformism of Boston's Yankee Protestant elite. Hicks opposed Boston "politicians" not because of any distaste for old fashioned patronage politics, but because she feels that Boston city government has not adequately represented the interests of her constituency. In her 1967 mayoralty campaign, she thus maintained that the main issue was "alienation:"

A powerful structure is coming into Boston to defeat the people. I'll take them all on.[15]

'People have felt alienated for a long time,' she said. 'And they've felt for a long time that I'm their voice in the city.'[16]

Bostonians are alienated, she believes, because Boston city government has ceded too much power to Massachusetts state government and to black civil rights leaders. In 1966, she accused Massachusetts state government of trying "to set up a dictatorship."[17] In 1967, she proudly asserted: "But I hope I am a symbol of resistance to civil rights leaders who do not represent the Negro parents of Boston. I will not appease."[18]

The Racial Imbalance Act and the 1967 riot became key elements in Hicks' campaign to prove to Bostonians their powerlessness over city government. In successful 1963 and 1965 reelection campaigns for the School Committee, she vehemently opposed the racial balancing of Boston public schools through bussing or any other "involuntary" means. During her 1967 campaign, Hicks often told audiences that politicians who favor school desegregation were giving preferential treatment to blacks: "I believe in civil rights. I don't believe in preferential rights."[19] Hicks also believed that city politicians gave unfair preference to blacks during the 1967 rioting. In her eyes, Boston police were shackled by politicians afraid of losing support among black voters:

'Instead of being told to enforce the law, police were under orders to avoid creating an incident,' Mrs. Hicks said. 'Law and order must be maintained in this city. The first rule of good government is law and order.'[20]

Louise Day Hicks pledged to combat the "alienation" of Boston's electorate by returning power to them through retaining neighborhood schools and increasing police authority.[21]

In Hicks' seven campaigns for elective office since 1963, she has repeatedly told audiences "you know where I stand." But where does Louise Day Hicks stand? Critics called her a "sly racist," and liberal columnist Tom Wicker saw her as embodying the northern white backlash. *Newsweek,* ridiculing Hicks and her supporters as Moon Mullins characters, maintained that with her 1967 mayoralty campaign the northern white "... backlash had come of age."[22] Her supporters are more likely than her opponents to oppose bussing, to oppose sending their children to predominantly black schools, and to resist racially integrating neighborhoods.[23] Hicks, however, stoutly maintains that she harbors no racist sentiments: "I challenge anyone to prove I've been anti-Negro either by word or action."[24] Her opposition to bussing, she says, is based not on racism but on concern for children: "I believe that little children should go to school in their own neighborhoods, with the children with whom they play. It is as simple as that."[25] Her calls for law and order, she asserts, represent only concern for the safety of all Boston citizens. Her voting record in the U.S. House similarly belies any facile categorization of her as conservative or liberal.[26] Perhaps, as she so forcefully avows, Louise Day Hicks is just trying to increase the political power wielded by Bostonians.

The Interview Schedule

Studying white attitudes on bussing and black rioting provides an opportunity to investigate Marxian and Weberian questions. Louise Day Hicks maintains that white attitudes toward these two issues are based on feelings of political powerlessness; in her eyes, the Boston white sees his lack of political power in the manner in which local and state governments have dealt with black rioting and the Racial Imbalance Act. Hicks implicitly employs a Weberian model: whites perceive themselves as politically powerless, but not necessarily as the possessors of low status or little economic power. Her assumptions, like those of Marx and Weber, cannot be accepted without empirical examination. The extent of overlap among the three dimensions remains to be tested; similarly, the effect of varying placement in the three dimensions on militancy remains to be tested.

Do Boston whites, as Louise Day Hicks believes, feel that they have little power over city government decisions on school bussing? Are these feelings of political powerlessness associated with feelings of more generalized political and economic powerlessness? Do those whites who feel powerless over school bussing decisions also believe that they have less status than other people? Do whites with blue-collar occupations have differing conceptions of their powerlessness than whites with white-collar occupations? Are feelings of social, economic, and political powerlessness associated with support for militant means? Are Boston whites who believe that the riots led to increased benefits and preferential treatment for blacks likely to employ similar means to attain their own ends? The survey conducted in September and October of 1970 offers some preliminary answers to these questions.

Interviews were conducted with 301 Boston adult white men.[a] The sample

---

[a] A description of the sampling and interviewing process is contained in Appendix A.

design was dictated by the desire both to maximize the number of respondents who support the use of militant means and to obtain a sample which would permit analysis of the effect of objective class on militancy. Since earlier research had demonstrated that militancy was greater among men, only men were included in the sample. Similarly, the sample was designed to yield similar proportions of middle and working class respondents.

The final study sample consisted of 138 white-collar men, 154 men with blue-collar occupations, and nine men who refused to divulge their occupations.[b] Sixty-one percent were not educated beyond high school; 18% had attended college; 12% were college graduates; and 8% had post-graduate training. Eighty-five percent of the 301 respondents were fully employed, and only 9% were retired.

Operationalizing the Variables

In designing questions and adapting questions from other surveys, we set a twofold goal. First, we tried to close the gap between theoretical and operational definitions of variables. We sought to include questions which would be closely related to the individual elements of the conceptual scheme; taken as a whole, we hoped that the interview schedule would include operationalizations of the major variables in the scheme, and would provide opportunities to examine key hypotheses. Second, we attempted to include questions which were theoretically relevant, situationally specific, and practically important. An empirical examination of militancy in the United States can provide interesting theoretical insights; yet such a survey, unless its questions focus on the political situation current in the area in which the survey is being conducted, can yield few findings of practical importance.

The next chapter will concentrate primarily upon three clusters of attitudinal variables: subjective and affective powerlessness along the class, status, and political power dimensions; militancy; and acquiescence. A brief review of the questions employed to measure these variables will allow readers to judge the extent to which the gap between theoretical and operational definitions has been narrowed, and the extent to which the questions achieve theoretical relevance, situational specificity, and practical importance.

Independent Variables: Subjective Cognitive and Affective Powerlessness. Particular care was taken in designing questions to measure the principal attitudinal independent variables: cognitive and affective perceptions of the individual's placement along the class, status, and political power dimensions. Few scholars have attempted to measure subjective perceptions of placement along all of Weber's three dimensions; even fewer investigators have attempted to

[b]A full list of respondent occupations is included in Appendix B.

employ parallel measures. Runciman includes a survey dealing with Weber's three dimensions in his *Relative Deprivation and Social Justice,* but he does not employ parallel measures.[27] In research reported during 1952, Hetzler employed parallel self-rating scales to measure the individual's perception of his position relative to others in the community along nine class and status hierarchies.[28]

Parallel questions for each of the three dimensions were designed by adapting Hadley Cantril's self-anchoring striving scale.[29] To determine the individual's perception of his position in the status dimension, the respondent was asked to identify his own rung and the rung of "people like yourself" on a general respect ladder. The top rung was identified as "those groups of people who are given the most respect," and the bottom rung was identified as representing "those given the least respect." Respondents were also asked to identify the ladder rungs occupied by eleven other groups: union members, Italians, medical doctors, Negroes, Irish, rich people, salesmen in a department store, people on welfare, construction workers, Jews, and police.[c] This procedure measures the rank of the individual relative to those at the top and bottom of the status dimension, and the individual's rank relative to those specific other groups. Subjective affective placement was tapped by asking:

Q. 17 — Would you say people like yourself get more respect than you deserve, just about the right amount of respect, or less respect than you deserve?

The person's perception of his placement in the political power dimension was measured in two ways. First, respondents ranked their own position and those of the other eleven groups on a ladder. The top rung represented "those groups of people which city officials pay the most attention to when making decisions on bussing school children," and the bottom rung represented "those groups which city officials pay the least attention to."[30] This question is thus specific to the school bussing, local governmental internal hierarchy of the subjective cognitive level of the political power dimension.[d] Second, respondents answered disagree-agree items adapted from standard political efficacy and political alienation scales.[31] Six of these items were employed to construct an additive index; each item in the index taps the individual's perception of his general political power and his power over governmental decision-making.[e] The additive index emerging from these six items will be taken as measuring the individual's placement on the subjective cognitive level of the general political power dimension. In addition, subjective affective political power was measured by Question 22: "In making decisions about school bussing, would you say city officials pay more attention than deserved to people like yourself, just about the right amount of attention, or less attention. . . . [than deserved]?"

---

[c]The subjective cognitive status question is reproduced in Appendix C.

[d]The subjective cognitive political power (bussing) question is reproduced in Appendix C.

[e]Item components of the general political power index are presented in Appendix C; intercorrelations are presented in Appendix D.

Using an adaptation of the Cantril self-anchoring striving scale identical to that employed in the status and political power items, we constructed parallel questions to measure the individual's self-placement on the subjective cognitive levels of the commodity, credit, and labor internal hierarchies of the economic dimension. However, a two stage pretest consisting of thirty interviews revealed an extreme tendency for respondents' self-rankings, and the rankings accorded to the other eleven groups, to cluster around the ladder midpoint. Because of insufficient differentiation among the groups, the ladder adaptation was abandoned and a simpler self-placement method was employed instead. For self-rankings on the labor internal hierarchy, respondents were asked:

Q. 44 – What about people like yourself? Would you say that people like yourself have a better chance than other people of getting a good job, about the same chance as other people, or a worse chance than other people?

In addition, those interviewed were also asked to identify which of the eleven groups has the best chance of obtaining good jobs and which the worst chance. Similar questions relating to recent layoffs and unemployment, and the commodity and credit internal hierarchies of the economic dimension were also employed.[32]

Dependent Variables: Militancy. Two series of structured questions, each relating to a different target, were used to measure militancy. The antigovernmental militancy measure consisted of an adaptation of several projective items designed by Matthews and Prothro.[33] Interviewers instructed respondents:

Q. 70 – Now, let's imagine that you have a child going to a school where there is nobody to help children get across a street crossing out in front. The crossing is dangerous, and one day a child is hit by a car. You think that somebody should be stationed at the crossing to help the children. So do your friends. But city officials aren't willing to do anything about it.

Respondents were then asked a series of thirteen questions concerning actions they might be willing to take to remedy this hypothetical situation; the actions ranged along a continuum from doing nothing to taking disruptive actions against City Hall.[34] Using Stouffer's H-technique, eleven of these items formed a seven point Guttman scale. The scale items are presented in Table 4-1.

A second series of items dealing with antiblack militancy were adapted from Morris and Jeffries' study of white reactions to the 1965 Watts riot. The questions focus on white willingness to use firearms for protection against black rioters and approval of the use of firearms against black rioters.[f]

Intervening Variables: Acquiescence. We hypothesized that the major determinant of militancy is not the individual's placement in the economic, status,

---

[f]Appendix C contains the antiblack militancy and white reactions to black rioting questions.

Table 4-1. Militancy Scale Items*

Scale Score	Question	Percentage of Respondents
0	Would not engage in any action.	8%
1	Yes – Q. 71: Would you write to city councilmen or other public officials to let them know how you feel about the crossing? AND/OR Yes – Q. 72: Would you contact your neighbors and friends to urge them to vote in a bloc for the city council candidate who promises to do something about the crossing?	11%
	AND	
2	Yes – Q. 73: Would you contribute money to the city council candidate who promises to do something about the crossing? AND/OR Yes – Q. 74: Would you attend rallies, dinners, or meetings for this candidate?	28%
	AND	
3	Yes – Q. 75: Would you march peaceably through town to bring the crossing to the attention of city officials?	26%
	AND	
4	Yes – Q. 77: Would you try to get publicity about the crossing by sitting-in at City Hall? AND/OR Yes – Q. 81: Would you go to a meeting where the Mayor was speaking and carry signs about the crossing?	16%
	AND	
5	Yes – Q. 78: Would you be willing to *talk* in favor of using disruptive tactics against City Hall – even if you don't really plan on doing anything violent? AND/OR Yes – Q. 80: Would you go to a meeting where the Mayor was speaking and boo him?	9%
	AND	
6	Yes – Q. 82: Would you go to a meeting where the Mayor was speaking and show your disapproval of his doing nothing about the crossing by throwing things at him – nothing that would hurt him? AND/OR Yes – Q. 79: Do you think you would *actually engage* in disruptive tactics against city property?	2%
		100% (N=299)†

Minimum Marginal Reproducibility = .73
Coefficient of Reproducibility = .95
Coefficient of Scalability= .81

*Scale computed through Stouffer's H-Technique. See: Samuel A. Stouffer, *Communism, Conformity, and Civil Liberties: A Cross-section of the Nation Speaks Its Mind* (New York: John Wiley and Sons, Inc., 1955), Appendix C; and Samuel A. Stouffer, Edgar F. Borgatta, David G. Hays, and Andrew F. Henry, "A Technique for Improving Cumulative Scales," *Public Opinion Quarterly*, Volume 16 (Summer 1952), pp. 273-91.

†Total excludes two (2) cases omitted because of missing values.

and political power dimensions, but rather his perception of whether the use of a certain means has been or is likely to be successful in achieving a particular end. The Bostonian's willingness to engage in disruptive tactics at City Hall because of governmental inattention to a dangerous school-crossing is not directly caused by his dissatisfaction with city government, but by his perception of whether disruptive tactics would lead government officials to improve the crossing. The person's willingness to counter-riot against blacks is not caused so much by his dissatisfactions with black riots and black demands, but by his perceptions of whether the riots have led to increased governmental benefits for blacks.

To measure the individual's perception of governmental acquiescence to militant tactics, a series of questions relating to the Roxbury riots and the school-crossing were employed. Regarding governmental acquiescence to Boston's black riots, our white respondents were asked:

Q. 32 – In the summer of 1967 there was a Negro riot in Roxbury. Do you think Roxbury has gotten a lot more help from the government since the riot, a little more help, or do they get about the same help now as they did before?

In conjunction with disruptive protests about the dangerous school-crossing, we queried:

Q. 84 – What do you think the Mayor would do if a sit-in protesting the school crossing were staged at City Hall? Do you think he would order the people arrested, try to ignore them, or would he try to do something about their demands?

The acquiescence questions were unidimensional and included no statements referring to approval of a particular end or approval of a particular means to achieve that end.

The worth of a survey rests largely upon the theoretical underpinnings of its research design, and on the relationship between the theoretical and operational definitions of variables. Survey research can contribute to the building and modification of comprehensive political theories. Yet in order to do so, the choice of questions for the interview schedule must be dictated by their relevance to the theoretical scheme being examined. In the next chapter, using our theoretically based questions, we will demonstrate how the results of the Boston survey can contribute to further modifying Marx's theorizing, as well as refining our own theoretical scheme.

5 Research Findings on Militancy

Marx and Engels were insistent on the 'scientific' character of Marxism in one essential respect: a critical social and historical theory had to subsume the findings and where necessary the methods of the advanced spheres of bourgeois thought – even where this last was not critical in intention, if extremely so in implication. Put in another way, Marxism at its origins was a chef d'oeuvre *[masterpiece] of bourgeois thought. . . .*[1]

Norman Birnbaum

Introduction

Three questions will be raised in this chapter. First, what are the relationships among self-perceived positions on the economic, status, and political power dimensions?[a] Marx believes that a person who sees himself as possessing high economic standing will also see himself as having equally high political power and status. Weber disagrees with Marx: a person who feels that he has high economic standing may also perceive himself as having little status and political power. Second, what attitudes are associated with white militancy? Marx predicts that militancy is not related to perceived economic, status, and political power positions, nor is it related to economic, status, and political power dissatisfactions and political ends. Rather, a person's willingness to take militant action is affected only by his perception of whether militant tactics will successfully accomplish the desired end. From Lipset and Bell's theorizing, we can infer a contrasting position: militancy derives in part from a person's dissatisfactions with his status.[2] Third, what is the effect of objective class on militancy? Are white-collar workers more or less militant than blue-collar workers?

Subjective Powerlessness: Do the Dimensions Overlap?

The key difference between Marx's and Weber's theorizing on militancy and

---

[a]In order to minimize clumsy wording, I will employ several terms interchangeably in this chapter. Self-perceived economic, status, and political power positions, perceived economic standing, status, and political power, and economic, status, and political power rankings are all used synonymously with the individual's position on the subjective cognitive level of the three dimensions. Status and political power dissatisfactions are used synonymously with the individual's position on the subjective affective level of the dimensions.

radicalism lies in their dissimilar definitions of class consciousness. For Marx, class consciousness is economic in genesis. The class conscious person perceives a large gap between himself and those at the top of the class structure. In Marx's eyes, economic class subsumes status and political power: the Boston white who perceives a large gap between himself and those at the top of the class structure will also perceive a large gap between himself and those at the top of the status and political power dimensions. Economic class, status, and political power are all but inseparable. Since they are practically inseparable, we gain nothing by conceptually or empirically distinguishing the three dimensions from each other.

Weber's theorizing leads to a different conclusion. The Boston white's economic standing is related to his status and political power. Yet the three dimensions do not necessarily overlap, and the relationships among the dimensions are historically specific. In 1871 Paris the worker's low economic standing might have been associated with little status and political power; but in 1971 Boston the worker's low economic standing might be associated with high status and great political power.

Do the dimensions overlap? An initial answer to this question emerges from Figure 5-1. While only 8% of the respondents in the Boston sample classify themselves within the lower segment of the status dimension, and only 11% regard themselves as low on the economic dimension, 30% of the respondents view themselves as possessing little political power over Boston city government's decisions on school bussing. Clearly, only limited overlap exists between the three dimensions. The substantially greater number of respondents holding lower positions on the political power dimension than on the status and economic dimensions indicates that some respondents who regard themselves as having little political power must view themselves as possessing higher ranks on the status and economic dimensions.

The relationships between the political, economic, and status dimensions must be more explicitly investigated if we are to determine whether white Bostonians' perceptions of their little influence over school bussing decisions are related to perceptions of low status and economic standing. If Marx was correct — if the individual's economic standing determines his status and his political power — then strong correlations will exist between perceived economic standing and perceived political power, and weaker correlations will exist between perceived status and perceived political power.

Weberian-oriented analysts of contemporary American politics, such as Lipset and Bell, speculate that Marx's theories provide an inadequate model for understanding recent American extremism. Unlike Marx, Lipset and Bell hypothesize that perceived status, and not just perceived economic standing, determines a person's perception of his political power. Lipset and Bell would predict that an equal correlation exists between status and political power self-perceptions as between economic and political power self-perceptions.

The correlations displayed in Table 5-1 suggest that both the Marxian and Weberian models provide partially accurate reflections of white Bostonians' views. As Marx would have suggested, the directions of the relationships are all

Figure 5-1 Subjective Cognitive Positions on Status, Political Power (Bussing), and Economic Dimensions*

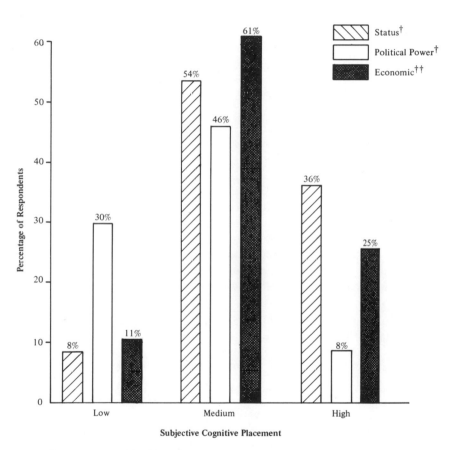

Table 5-1. Correlations (Gamma) Between Subjective Cognitive Positions on Status, Political, and Economic Dimensions*

	Status	Political (Bussing)	Political† (General)	Economic
Status	–	+.12	+.15	+.26
Political (Bussing)		–	+.33	+.05
Political (General)			–	+.19
Economic				–

* For the status and political power (bussing internal hierarchy) dimensions, the responses were collapsed as described in Figure 5-1. For discussion of the use of Gamma, see Appendix E.

† The general political power dimension is the additive political power (alienation) index described in Chapter 4 and in Appendix D. Using more conventional terminology, a low position on the general political power dimension is equivalent to a high position on political alienation. The index was collapsed through dichotomizing at the median.

positive: people who classify themselves as high on one dimension are slightly more likely to classify themselves as high on the other dimensions. Yet beyond this minimal confirmation of the Marxian model, the data indicate that the Weberian model provides better insights into 1970 white Boston than does the Marxian model. None of the relationships are particularly strong, and none approach the perfect correlations that the pure Marxian model posits. Weber was right: class, status, and political power are both conceptually and empirically distinct.

Table 5-1 lends weak preliminary support to Lipset and Bell's hypothesizing. Self-perceived economic position is only trivially associated with perceived political power over local government school bussing decisions, and weakly associated with perceptions of general political power. Perceived status emerges as a more stable, although nevertheless quite weak, predictor of perceived political power. In fact, the average correlation between perceived status and the political power hierarchies (+.14) is a tiny bit higher than the average correlation between perceived economic position and the political power hierarchies (+.12).[b] These differences are minimal. Nonetheless, they do indicate that Marx's class consciousness concept may need revising. The three dimensions are clearly empirically distinct, and the data fail to bear out Marx's assumption of the primacy of the economic dimension. Rather, perceived economic position predicts perceived political power no better than does perceived status.

Why do the Boston data not correspond with Marx's hypothesizing?

[b]Data to be presented later in this chapter will more strongly indicate the relative importance of the status dimension.

Although we will attempt to answer this question more fully in Chapter 6, some preliminary speculation can profitably occur here. The scholar who rigidly adheres to Marxian ideology would maintain that Marx was not wrong. Such a scholar would quote Marx's famous 1881 comment to Vera Zasulich: "everything depends on the historical environment in which it occurs."[3] Or perhaps the Marxist ideologue would admiringly quote Engels' 1890 letter to Joseph Bloch:

According to the materialist conception of history the determining element in history is *ultimately* the production and reproduction [of capital] in real life. More than this neither Marx nor I have ever asserted. If therefore somebody twists this into the statement that the economic element is the *only* determining one, he transforms it into a meaningless, abstract and absurd phrase. The economic situation is the basis, but the various elements of the super-structure . . . . also exercise their influence upon the course of the historical struggles and in many cases preponderate in determining their *form.*[4]

If either of these two quotes escape him, the ideologue might retreat behind the time-honored Marxist shield against revisionism, and claim that our blue- and white-collar respondents are the hapless victims of false consciousness. Such attempts to guard Marxian theoretical honor must be dismissed as ideological defenses. Although the equal importance of the status dimension with the economic dimension might reflect false consciousness or American exceptionalism, the questions raised by our findings cannot be adequately answered through such facile application of Marxist dogma.

A plausible explanation may lie in the nature of traditional Americanism ideology.[5] Immigrants to the United States, such as the parents of 47% of our sample who were born outside of the United States, were confronted with an Americanism ideology containing two key elements. First, the Americanism ideology stressed the presence of economic opportunity: all Americans, regardless of their economic or social standing, supposedly possess an equal chance for upward economic mobility. Second, the Americanism ideology emphasized that "all men are created equal;" created equal not in their economic standing or natural ability, but in their inherent good and the respect which should be accorded to them because of that inherent good. The Americanism ideology did not posit economic equality as a reality or as a goal, but rather as a potential reality. Yet the Americanism ideology did stress status equality as a reality: regardless of their diverse economic standings or dissimilar natural abilities, all Americans were to receive equal respect. Economic differentiation was accepted as basic to American life; status differentiation was assumed to be absent.

Obviously, both status and economic differentiation exist among Boston's whites. Some of the interviewed whites classify themselves as possessing high status or economic standing, while other respondents regard themselves as holding low status or economic standing. Approximately equal proportions classed themselves as low on the economic and on the status dimensions; why then should perceived economic power be no more important than perceived status as a predictor of perceived political power? If our review of the Americanism ideology is accepted as plausible, then one could argue that the Bostonian who classes himself as low on the economic dimension — even if he is dissatisfied with that position — might accept this low position as just; perhaps not as individually just, but certainly as just in terms of not refuting the Americanism ideology and not reflecting basic inadequacies in the American social structure. Yet the Bostonian who perceives himself as low in status would regard this position as basically unjust, and as a reflection of a gap between the American social structure and the myths posited by the Americanism ideology. If a gap exists between the undifferentiated status of the Americanism ideology and the differentiated status of the contemporary American social structure, then the social structure itself would be regarded as unjust or the ideology as absurd. Following Weber's logic, one could then reason that these conceptions of structural inadequacies, stemming from perceptions of low status, would be transposed into feelings of political powerlessness.

Cognitive Placement of Other Groups on the Dimensions

These findings leave important questions unanswered: Do white Bostonians differentiate between the status possessed by other groups in Boston? Do they believe that different groups have dissimilar political power over city government decisions on school bussing? Are groups that are regarded as having little status also believed to have little political power?

Figure 5-2 graphically displays the mean status and political power ladder rungs accorded to the twelve groups classified by the interviewed Boston white men. Negroes and people on welfare, according to our respondents, have the least status; our respondents regard medical doctors and rich people as the two groups with the highest status. Turning to the political power ladder, we find a marked reversal of group positions. Negroes and people on welfare, the two groups given the lowest status, are perceived as possessing relatively great political power over Boston city government decisions on bussing school children. Negroes, given the second lowest position on the status ladder, are regarded as holding the most political power; people on welfare, the lowest group on the status ladder, fall among the four groups regarded as having the most political power over bussing decisions.

Another perspective on the differences between the status and the political power dimensions can be gained by investigating Figure 5-3, which graphs the percentage of our white respondents placing blacks on various rungs of the status and political power ladders. Over 50% of the interviewed Boston whites think that blacks fall on the bottom three rungs of the nine rung status ladder; yet when classifying blacks on the nine rung bussing political power ladder, only 12% of these same respondents view blacks as falling in the bottom three rungs. Indeed, Figure 5-3 illustrates that *one-half* of the respondents feel that blacks

Figure 5-2 Average Status and Political Power (Bussing) Ladder Rungs

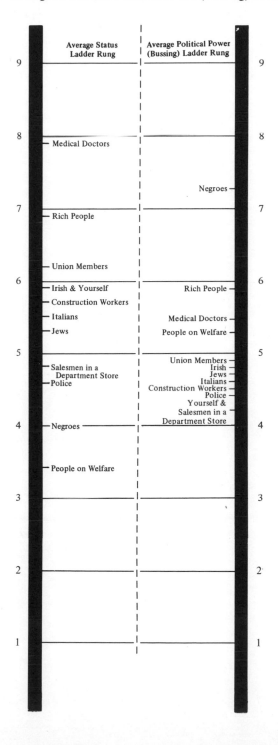

Figure 5-3 Negro Status and Political Power (Bussing) Ladder Rungs.

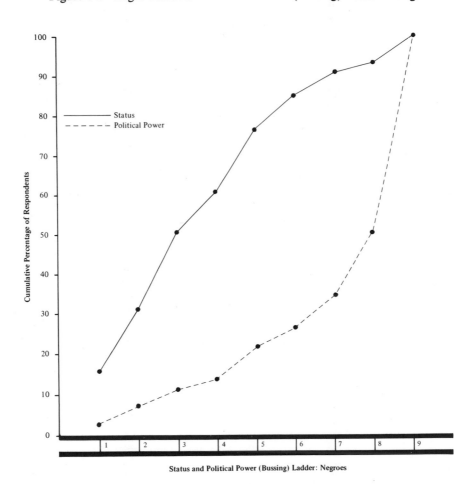

Status and Political Power (Bussing) Ladder: Negroes

occupy the *single highest rung* on the bussing political power ladder!

How do the interviewed Boston whites see their status and political power relative to the status and political power of blacks? By taking the difference between the ladder rung on which the respondent placed himself, and the ladder rung on which he placed blacks, we can obtain such a relative picture. Figure 5-4 graphs the magnitude of the difference between the rung occupied by the respondent on the status and political power ladders, and the rung which he accorded to blacks on each ladder. A respondent placing himself on rung one (lowest position) of the bussing political power ladder and placing blacks on rung nine (highest position) of the bussing political power ladder would thus receive a *-8* political power relative deprivation score; a person placing himself on the same status rung with blacks would thus receive a *0* status relative deprivation score. Few interviewed Bostonians feel that they are deprived in terms of status relative to Negroes; only 15% of these men regard themselves as possessing less status than blacks. Yet a totally different picture of relative deprivation emerges when we turn to bussing political power. While status relative deprivation does not characterize the sample, political power relative deprivation is all pervasive. Of these Boston white men, 80% believe that blacks wield more political power over city government bussing decisions than themselves; only 8% regard themselves as having more power than blacks on this highly charged political issue.

Is there a factual basis for white beliefs that they have relatively little political power over Boston city government decisions on school bussing? Only minimal progress has been made in integrating Boston's public schools. In those few schools where city generated desegregation attempts have occurred, redistricting of school boundaries – and not bussing – has been the usual means of racially balancing the student body. The Boston School Committee has continually resisted State Board of Education demands that de facto school segregation be eliminated. Boston resistance has been so great that millions of dollars in state education funds have been withheld from Boston because of noncompliance with the Massachusetts Racial Imbalance Act. The recent history of Boston government's resistance to desegregating the public schools, coupled with the 30% of the respondents who regard themselves as having little influence over city government decisions on school bussing and the 80% who feel that blacks wield more power than themselves on this issue, indicates that a gap exists between the reality of the Boston situation – a situation in which public officials have taken care not to lose white support – and white perceptions of the situation. Louise Day Hicks may have been wrong in maintaining that Boston whites have little power over city government decisions on school bussing, but she was right in asserting that many Boston whites think that they have little power over such decisions.

Why do the interviewed Boston whites think that they have less political power than blacks over city government decisions on school bussing? Perhaps our respondents are reacting to state and federal initiatives against the Boston school system. Boston whites may feel that school bussing decisions will be

Figure 5-4 Cognitive Status and Political Power (Bussing) Relative Deprivation

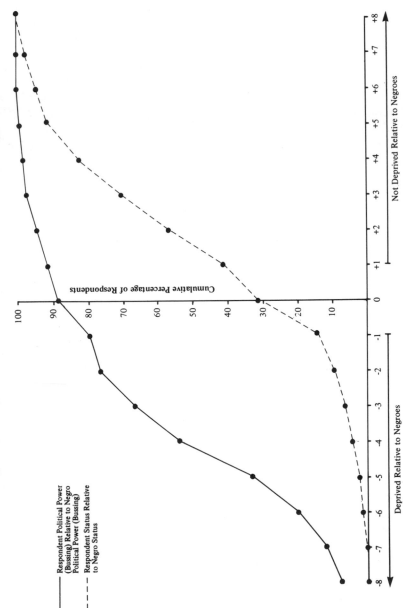

made not at the city government level, but at the state or federal level. Boston whites may assert that they have little influence over city government decisions on school bussing, because they may believe that decision-making power over local schools does not rest in the local government. Further, our white respondents may think that blacks have substantial influence on desegregation decisions at the more important state and federal levels.

Subjective Cognitive Powerlessness and Subjective Affective Powerlessness

In his writings on class consciousness and political action, Karl Marx inadequately distinguishes between the working man's knowledge of his relatively disadvantaged position in the objective class structure, his dissatisfaction with his position, and political actions taken to alter the class structure and enhance his position in it. In Marx's mind, the worker who becomes aware of his disadvantaged position will become dissatisfied, and the dissatisfied worker will take revolutionary political action to undermine the class structure. Max Weber, on the other hand, implies a contrasting position: knowledge is distinct from dissatisfaction, and dissatisfaction is distinct from action.

In our Marxian-Weberian theoretical schema, we speculated that cognitive perceptions of a low position on any dimension would be closely related to affective placement on that dimension: the white Bostonian who sees himself as possessing little political power will also tend to be dissatisfied with his lack of political power. However, remembering Weber's theorizing, we also speculated that the relationship will be far from perfect. Table 5-2, which displays correlations between subjective cognitive and subjective affective positions, supports this speculation. As we predicted, the bulk of the correlations are

Table 5-2. Correlations (Gamma) Between Subjective Cognitive Positions and Subjective Affective Positions*

	Subjective Cognitive Position			
	Status	Political (Bussing)	Political (General)	Economic
Subjective Affective Position				
Status	+.57	+.29	+.48	+.23
Political (Bussing)	+.01	+.71	+.18	+.03

* Subjective cognitive levels collapsed as described in Figure 5-1.

positive but far from perfect; in all eight cases, respondents who perceive their position as low on the status, political power, or economic dimensions are also somewhat likely to be dissatisfied with their status or political power. Further, as we also would have predicted, the two strongest correlations are between perceived status and status dissatisfaction, and between perceived bussing political power and bussing political power dissatisfaction. Knowledge and dissatisfaction are indeed related to each other, but knowledge and dissatisfaction are also conceptually and empirically distinct.

The data on cognitive and affective powerlessness presented in this section lend evidence for the need to re-evaluate Marx's theorizing. Marx would have asserted that total overlap occurs between the political, status, and economic dimensions, and that a perfect correlation exists between cognitive and affective positions on each dimension. But we have discovered that total overlap does not exist among the dimensions, and that cognitive and affective placements are not perfectly correlated with each other. The Weberian perspective, which analytically and empirically separates the three dimensions and the three levels within each dimension, more accurately reflects 1970 Boston than does Marx's framework.

Militancy and Its Determinants

White Backlash and White Militancy

Discussions of urban politics during the mid- and late-1960's often involved speculation on the existence and ingredients of the white backlash. According to *Newsweek,* white backlash was embodied in the white ethnic appeals and rigid antibussing stance of Boston's Louise Day Hicks.[6] Hicks' 1967 candidacy for the Boston mayoralty, and George Wallace's 1968 presidential candidacy, were seen by commentators as testing-grounds for America's whites; the poor showings of both Hicks and Wallace were interpreted by some as evidence that white backlash was not as prevalent as had been supposed.

What was the white backlash? Reactions to three 1960's political phenomena were viewed as its essential ingredients: increased governmental concern for blacks, black riots, and student protests over the Vietnam War. Closely connected to reactions to these three phenomena was what Jerome H. Skolnick terms white militancy: white willingness to use violent and unconventional political means in achieving their ends.[7]

Massive political changes have occurred since the 1969 advent of the Nixon administration. Presidential rhetoric no longer focuses on improving the lot of America's blacks, black riots have subsided, and Vietnam protests have declined. Governmental benefits for blacks, black riots, and Vietnam no longer dominate American political discourse. Has the removal of the motives behind white backlash and militancy affected its incidence? Louise Day Hicks — supposedly the personification of the white backlash — lost to Kevin White in the 1967 Boston mayoralty campaign by 7% of the votes; opposing White once again in the 1971 mayoralty, Hicks lost by 24% of the votes.[8] If Louise Day Hicks embodies the white backlash in Boston, then it appears that the backlash has ebbed.

Or perhaps Boston's white backlash and militancy were never as prevalent as had been thought. A comparison of responses to four questions concerning reactions to black rioting, included in both the 1965 Los Angeles study and the 1970 Boston survey, suggests that white militancy targeted against the black population may have been less prevalent in Boston than in other cities. Table 5-3 indicates that on all four common indicators, the reaction to black rioting among the white Boston men interviewed was substantially less severe than

Table 5-3. Comparison of White Reaction and White Militancy in Los Angeles and Boston

Question*		Positive Response	
		Los Angeles (Males and Females 1965†)	Boston (White Males 1970††)
White Reaction			
"During the time of the (riot), did you feel fear for yourself or your family's safety?"	Great Deal 23% ⎫ 55% Some 32% ⎭		40%
"Did you approve of white people buying guns to protect themselves during the (riot)?"	Yes	57%	38%
White Militancy			
"Did you, at any time, consider using firearms to protect yourself or your family?"	Yes	29%	14%
"Did you buy firearms or ammunition to protect yourself or your family?"	Yes	5%	3%

* The questions here were used in the Los Angeles study. The Boston questions were based on the Los Angeles questions, but the wording was slightly modified. See questions 34, 35, 36, 37 in Appendix C.

† Morris and Jeffries, *op. cit.*, pp. 486-7. Percentages based on full sample of 583 which includes "don't knows" and "not ascertained."

†† Percentages based on full sample of 301 and includes "don't knows" and "not ascertained."

among the Los Angeles respondents. Particularly interesting are the differences between the cities on those questions where answers concerning solely white reaction are elicited, and on those questions where answers dealing with militant actions are elicited. Although the white reaction among the 1970 Boston respondents appears to have been less harsh than among the 1965 Los Angeles respondents, a greater disparity exists between the militancy of the Boston and the Los Angeles respondents: militancy is almost twice as great in Los Angeles.[c]

Why should Boston differ from Los Angeles? Three answers could be given to this question. First, one might answer that no difference really exists between Boston and Los Angeles. The Boston survey was conducted in 1970 — two years after Boston's rioting had ended. The Los Angeles study was conducted in 1965 — following closely in the aftermath of the Watts rebellion. Perhaps the differences are due to the passage of time. The rioting may have faded from the memories of our Boston respondents; along with fading memories, come lessened backlash and militancy. But this fails to explain the differences between the incidence of white reaction and the prevalence of white militancy. Why should the differences between the Boston and Los Angeles respondents be greater on the militancy than on the reaction questions?

The political scientist who prefers political cultural explanations might offer a second answer. Boston has long been the home of vociferous civil libertarians. Thoreau and Welch lived and worked in the Boston area. Perhaps elite civil libertarian concerns have permeated the mass political culture of Boston. If this were true, then we might expect Bostonians to be more sympathetic than others to the black riots, to have less harsh reactions, to be less likely to take militant actions against blacks, and to approve more strongly of black protests. Somewhat similar questions concerning black civil rights tactics and militancy, asked of the Boston and Los Angeles respondents (Table 5-4), reveals that Bostonians in 1970 were no more sympathetic towards the black riots than Los Angelenos in 1965. Eighteen percent of the 1965 Los Angeles respondents approved of the use of various militant political means by blacks, and only 8% of the 1970 Boston respondents maintained that Negroes were "right in rioting." In addition to casting some doubt on the validity of the political cultural explanation, Table 5-4 leads us further away from the time-lag explanation presented above. If the riots had faded from the memories of the white Bostonians interviewed in 1970, why are they equally as opposed to black militancy as were the 1965 Los Angeles respondents?

A third answer lies in our Marxian-Weberian theoretical framework. The interviewed Bostonians are no less antagonistic than the interviewed Los Angelenos to the riots. Yet antiblack militancy among the Boston respondents

---

[c]Morris and Jeffries' data also include females, whereas our data do not. Morris and Jeffries include few tabulations by sex; however, these few tabulations indicate that Los Angeles female respondents are considerably less militant than Los Angeles male respondents. Thus, 37% of the interviewed Los Angeles white men considered using firearms, but only 22% of the interviewed women considered using firearms (Morris and Jeffries, *op. cit.,* p. 503). These data indicate that Los Angeles white men are even more militant than Boston white men than is indicated by Tables 5-3 and 5-4.

Table 5-4. **Comparison of White Approval of Black Militancy in Los Angeles and Boston**

	Los Angeles (White Males and Females 1965*)		Boston (White Males 1970)
"People have expressed many different opinions as to the best methods or strategies that Negroes should use in getting their rights. Would you tell me which one of these statements of strategy you most agree with?			Do you think that the people in Roxbury:
— The civil rights movement should be stopped completely. Negroes already have their rights, enough or more than is due them.	5%		— Should . . . have waited patiently for the government to do something to help them.
— There is no need for the civil rights movement. Things should be allowed to take their natural course.	7%	12%	19%
— Negroes should stop pushing so hard. Things should be improved step-by-step in a gradual manner through political or legal means.		68%	— Should . . . have used other tactics to protest in a more peaceful way. 68%
— Negroes should keep the pressure on and keep it in front of the public eye with sit-ins and demonstrations.	17%		
— Negroes should be willing to use violent methods to get their rights if nonviolence won't do it."	1%	18%	— Were justified in rioting. 8%
NA/DK		2%	5%
Total		100% (583)	100% (301)

* Morris and Jeffries, *op. cit.*, p. 511.

was less frequent. The relatively complacent reaction in Boston to the 1967 riot can be accounted for by comparing the Roxbury and the Watts riots. In Watts, thirty-four people were killed; in Roxbury, nobody died.[9] The severity of the Watts riot may have led Los Angeles whites to believe that the city government should have taken even stronger measures to quell the rioting. The frequent looting and widespread property damage which occurred during the 1965 Watts riot may have led to white belief that the Los Angeles city government acquiesced to the violent means employed by the black rioters. The less frequent looting and less massive property damage occurring during the 1967 Roxbury riot may have led Boston whites to think that the city government did not acquiesce to the black rioters. Building upon the logic of Chapter 3, we can suggest that belief in governmental acquiescence to violent means led to greater militancy. Los Angeles whites, thinking that the city government had acquiesced, would be more militant; Boston whites, thinking that their government had not acquiesced, would be less militant.

At this point, we can only speculate on the effect of perceived acquiescence on militancy. The data on the relationship between militancy and acquiescence will be presented shortly. These data will show that the explanation arising from the cross-city comparisons is quite plausible: men who think that the government acquiesces to violent or unconventional tactics are more militant.

Powerlessness and Militancy

A purely utilitarian conception of political means forms the basis of the Marxian acquiescence hypothesis. The assumption lying behind the acquiescence hypothesis is that people rationally decide whether a particular means will achieve a desired end.[10] If the means is regarded as having been successful in another situation, if the means is judged as likely to be successful in another situation, or if the means is judged as likely to be successful in the current situation, then it will be employed. The Boston leftist is no more likely to use violent means than the Boston conservative; the Bostonian who feels he has little status and political power, or a low economic standing, is no more likely to favor violent means than the Bostonian who sees himself as possessing great status and political power, as well as a high economic standing.

Table 5-5. Correlations (Gamma) Between Subjective Cognitive Positions and Militancy

	Subjective Cognitive Position			
	Status	Political (Bussing)	Political (General)	Economic
Militancy				
Antiblack Militancy	+.17	−.08	−.41	+.01
Antigovernmental Militancy	−.17	+.05	+.04	+.13

Some early evidence about the worth of the acquiescence hypothesizing emerges from Table 5-5, which specifies the correlations between militancy and subjective cognitive positions. The correlations between antigovernmental militancy and subjective cognitive positions are inconsistent in direction, and either weak or trivial in strength. While those who see themselves as low in status are more likely to take militant action against the government, those who perceive their economic position as high are also slightly more likely militantly to oppose the government. Turning to antiblack militancy, we again find correlations mixed in strength and direction. Among the subjective cognitive items, status and general political power constitute the two best predictors of antiblack militancy; perceived status is weakly positively associated with antiblack militancy, and perceived general political power is strongly negatively associated with willingness to take militant actions targeted against Boston's blacks.

The data presented in Table 5-5 can lead to no firm conclusions about the validity of the acquiescence hypothesizing. The hypothesizing predicts that no relationship exists between subjective cognitive positions and militancy. In four of the eight cases, the trivial strength of the relationships totally supports the hypothesizing; in three of the remaining four cases, the relationships are weak and thus present no sturdy evidence either for or against the hypothesizing. The substantial directional inconsistency also indicates that economic, status, and political power self-perceptions are not stable predictors of militancy. Such directional inconsistency supports the acquiescence hypothesizing. Yet general political power emerges as a relatively strong predictor of antiblack militancy; this finding is at odds with the acquiescence hypothesis.

If the correlations between subjective cognitive positions and militancy are mixed in strength and direction, then we would expect similar inconsistency in the correlations between subjective affective positions and militancy. Yet Tables 5-6 and 5-7, which detail the relationships between dissatisfactions and antiblack militancy, and Tables 5-8 and 5-9, which specify the relationships between dissatisfactions and antigovernmental militancy, reveal only one such incon- sistency. All of the correlations are negative: interviewed Boston white men who are dissatisfied with their status and political power over city government decisions on school bussing are more likely to take militant action against both blacks and the government. With the single exception of the relationship between political power dissatisfactions and antigovernmental militancy, the correlations are also all relatively strong.

These findings are contrary to the acquiescence hypothesizing; they thus require further scrutiny. By comparing Tables 5-6 and 5-7 to Tables 5-8 and 5-9, we see that status dissatisfactions are a more stable predictor of militancy than political power dissatisfactions; status dissatisfactions are also somewhat more strongly associated with both antigovernmental and antiblack militancy than are political power dissatisfactions. Respondents who maintain that they receive "less respect than they deserve" are almost twice as likely to have considered using guns to protect themselves during the Roxbury riot than respondents who think that they have enough or too much status. Similarly, respondents who are

Table 5-6. Subjective Affective Status and Antiblack Militancy

| | Subjective Affective Status* | |
| | Would you say people like yourself get: | |
	Less respect than you deserve (N = 39)	Just about the right amount of respect/and more respect than you deserve (N = 229)
Antiblack Militancy		
At any time during the [1967 Roxbury] riot did you *consider* using a gun to protect yourself or your family?		
Did *not* consider using a gun	74%	86%
Did consider using a gun	26	14
	100%	100%
	G = −.38	

* D.K.'s and N.A.'s excluded. See Appendix E.

Table 5-7. Subjective Affective Political Power (Bussing) and Antiblack Militancy

| | Subjective Affective Political Power (Bussing)* | |
| | In making decisions about school bussing, would you say city officials pay: | |
	Less attention [than deserved to people like yourself] (N = 115)	Just about the right amount of attention/and more attention than deserved to people like yourself (N = 119)
Antiblack Militancy		
At any time during the [1967 Roxbury] riot did you *consider* using a gun to protect yourself or your family?		
Did *not* consider using a gun	81%	90%
Did consider using a gun	19	10
	100%	100%
	G = −.36	

* D.K.'s and N.A.'s excluded. See Appendix E.

Table 5-8. Subjective Affective Status and Antigovernmental Militancy

	Subjective Affective Status*	
	Would you say people like yourself get:	
	Less respect than you deserve	Just about the right amount of respect/and more respect than you deserve
	(N = 42)	(N = 241)

Antigovernmental Militancy

		Less respect	Right amount
Low	0	2%	9%
	1	5	13
	2	24	28
	3	24	27
	4	24	15
	5	19	7
High	6	2	2
		100%	101%†

G = −.37

* D.K.'s and N.A.'s excluded. See Appendix E.
† Deviation from 100% due to rounding.

Table 5-9. Subjective Affective Political Power (Bussing) and Antigovernmental Militancy

	Subjective Affective Political Power (Bussing)*	
	In making decisions about school bussing, would you say city officials pay:	
	Less attention [than deserved to people like yourself]	Just about the right amount of attention/and more attention than deserved to people like yourself
	(N = 123)	(N = 123)

Antigovernmental Militancy

		Less attention	Right amount
Low	0	6%	7%
	1	8	14
	2	29	26
	3	29	24
	4	15	19
	5	8	10
High	6	4	0
		99%†	100%

G = −.08

* D.K.'s and N.A.'s excluded. See Appendix E.
† Deviation from 100% due to rounding.

dissatisfied with their status are twice as likely to fall within the three highest scalar positions on antigovernmental militancy than those who are satisfied with their status. Unlike status dissatisfaction, political power dissatisfaction is unevenly associated with antiblack and antigovernmental militancy. While a relatively strong inverse relationship exists between political power satisfaction and antiblack militancy, only a weak inverse relationship exists between political power satisfaction and antigovernmental militancy.

Three questions emerge from these findings. First, why are status dissatisfactions a stronger and more stable predictor of militancy than political power dissatisfactions? Second, why are political power dissatisfactions more strongly associated with antiblack than antigovernmental militancy? And third, what are the effects of these findings on our acquiescence hypothesizing?

Status discontents within the contemporary United States, as was pointed out earlier, are basically structural dissatisfactions: the respondent who classifies himself as receiving less status than he deserves will angrily blame his own lack of status on the American socio-political structure. Respondents who are dissatisfied with their status are therefore also likely to be dissatisfied with the American socio-political structure. Political power dissatisfactions, on the other hand, are not necessarily transposed into discontent with the structure of American society. The respondent who regards himself as possessing little political power may blame this either on failings within the socio-political structure, *or* on actions taken by other groups which might diminish his own political power. Whatever their source, structural discontents are more likely than other discontents to be transposed into radicalism and militancy, both of which involve affecting the socio-political structure. Status discontents per se do not lead to militancy; rather, the structural nature of status discontents leads to militancy. Since status discontents are more likely than political discontents to be structural in nature, status discontents are more strongly associated with militancy.

Why are political dissatisfactions more strongly associated with antiblack than with antigovernmental militancy? The answer lies in the internal differentiation within the political power dimension. The question concerning political power dissatisfactions which was asked of the Boston respondents dealt with school bussing. The racially related political power dissatisfaction question is more in line with the antiblack militancy measure (centering on whether the respondent considered using guns to protect himself during the 1967 Roxbury riot) than with the antigovernmental militancy scale (centering on nonrace related projective questions about actions protesting a dangerous school-crossing). If a political power dissatisfaction measure had been designed that bore a closer conceptual relationship to the antigovernmental militancy scale, then a stronger correlation might have emerged.

What are the effects of these findings on the acquiescence hypothesizing? Until we examine the relationship between acquiescence and militancy, we can only conjecture on what revisions are needed in our Marxian-Weberian theoretical scheme. Yet these preliminary data do indicate that the acquiescence hypothesizing requires revision. Contrary to our earlier theorizing, status and political power dissatisfactions predict militancy.

Ends and Militancy

Like the hypothesizing on the lack of a relationship between dissatisfactions and militancy, the data reveal that the hypothesizing on the lack of a relationship between ends and means requires revision. In Table 5-10, a question on approval of the 1967 Roxbury riot (ends) is cross-tabulated with whether the individual

Table 5-10. Ends and Antiblack Militancy

	Ends*		
	Do you think that the people in Roxbury:		
	Should have waited patiently for the government to do something to help them	Should . . . have used other tactics to protest in a more peaceful way	Were justified in rioting
	(N = 54)	(N = 197)	(N = 21)
Antiblack Militancy			
At any time during the riot did you *consider* using a gun to protect yourself or your family?			
Did *not* consider using a gun	76%	87%	95%
Did consider using a gun	24	13	5
	100%	100%	100%
		G = −.40	

* D.K.'s and N.A.'s excluded. See Appendix E.

considered using guns to protect himself against blacks during the riot (means). A clear inverse relationship exists between riot approval and militancy. Five percent of the respondents who believed that blacks were "right in rioting" considered using guns for protection, 13% of the respondents who thought that blacks "should have used more peaceful tactics" considered using guns, and 24% of the respondents who asserted that blacks "should have waited for the government to act" considered using guns. Rather than no meaningful correlation between means and ends, a relatively strong relationship exists. The conventional wisdom seems to be correct; people who strongly oppose rioters' ends are most likely to employ violent means to express their opposition.

The utilitarian calculus of the Marxian-Weberian theoretical scheme is only partially correct. The white Bostonian's choice of political means may be affected by his calculation of whether the government will acquiesce to a particular means, but it is also influenced by whether he holds extreme views. We can speculate that people who are dissatisfied and who disapprove of the 1967 riot hold these views more intensely than do satisfied and approving people. Our Marxian-Weberian hypothesizing is based upon the assumption that intensity is randomly distributed along the continuum of ends. Put in another way, the hypothesizing assumes that people with extreme (disapproving) ends are no more or less likely to hold these views with great intensity than people with moderate ends; holding the intensity of views constant, ends would not vary with means. Yet if intensity does vary with ends, and if extreme views are held more intensely than moderate views, then people with more extreme views might be more likely to engage in militant actions. The relationship between dissatisfactions, riot disapproval, and militancy might be indirect, and only a reflection of a direct relationship between intensity of views and militancy.[11]

Acquiescence and Militancy

The relationship between acquiescence and militancy forms the basis of Marxian theorizing on political action. A person's political ends determine his choice of a target, but a person's perception of which actions will succeed determines his choice of militant or nonmilitant means for affecting the chosen target. The data discussed above reveal that the utilitarian calculus posited by the Marxian theoretical scheme provides only a partially accurate reflection of the relationships between dissatisfactions, ends, and militancy. However, it is nonetheless possible that acquiescence, in addition to dissatisfactions and ends, predicts militancy.

Acquiescence and Militancy

Does perceived acquiescence directly affect militancy? Tables 5-11 and 5-12 indicate that the answer is yes. As predicted, the Boston white man who perceives the government as acquiescing to militant means is more willing to use those means himself than the person who perceives the government as not acquiescing. Looking at antiblack militancy (Table 5-11), we find that respondents who agree with the acquiescent response that "Roxbury has gotten a lot more help from the government since the riot" are three times more militant that other respondents. A similar, although much weaker, relationship exists between perceived acquiescence and antigovernmental militancy (Table 5-12). Investigating the top three scalar positions, we find that those respondents

Table 5-11. Perceived Acquiescence and Antiblack Militancy

	Perceived Acquiescence*		
	In the summer of 1967 there was a Negro riot in Roxbury. Do you think:		
	[Roxbury gets] about the same help now as [it] did before? (N = 64)	[Roxbury gets] a little more help [now] (N = 76)	Roxbury has gotten a lot more help from the government since the riot (N = 104)
Antiblack Militancy			
At any time during the riot did you *consider* using a gun to protect yourself or your family?			
Did consider using a gun	92%	92%	77%
Did *not* consider using a gun	8	8	23
	100%	100%	100%
		G = +.47	

* D.K.'s and N.A.'s excluded. See Appendix E.

Table 5-12. Perceived Acquiescence and Antigovernmental Militancy

	Perceived Acquiescence*		
	What do you think the Mayor would do if a sit-in protesting the school crossing were staged at City Hall? Do you think he would:		
	Order the people arrested (N = 20)	Try to ignore them (N = 79)	Try to do something about their demands (N = 169)
Antigovernmental Militancy			
Low ↑ 0	25%	8%	5%
1	20	9	11
2	25	28	29
3	10	33	24
4	20	11	19
5	0	10	10
High ↓ 6	0	1	2
	100%	100%	100%
		G = +.15	

* D.K.'s and N.A.'s excluded. See Appendix E.

who believe that the Mayor would try to meet the protestors' demands are 50% more militant than respondents who think that the Mayor would not acquiesce to the protestors.

Tables 5-11 and 5-12 reveal that perceived acquiescence is much more strongly associated with antiblack than with antigovernmental militancy. The differing magnitudes of the two relationships may indicate that perceptions of past governmental acquiescence are more likely to lead to militancy than perceptions of future governmental acquiescence. The governmental acquiescence to black rioters question was specifically tied to actual governmental help since the 1967 Roxbury riot, while the governmental acquiescence to school-crossing protestors measure was a projective question in which respondents were asked to imagine the Mayor's response to a sit-in protesting the situation. The riots question measured perceived past acquiescence, while the school-crossing question measured perceived future acquiescence.

The difference between past and future acquiescence should be juxtaposed with the earlier speculation concerning the group to which the government is perceived as acquiescing. We theorized that the Bostonian who perceives the government as acquiescing to militant action — whether the action has been employed by himself, by another group with similar ends to his own, or by another group with ends dissimilar to his own — will be more likely to utilize militant means than the Bostonian who does not regard the government as acquiescing to militant means. The relationships between acquiescence to riots, acquiescence to a dangerous school-crossing protest, and militancy indicate that the earlier speculation on the source of the militant action was correct. Even where disagreement exists with the ends which the militant actions were used to accomplish, as in the case of the Roxbury rioting, perceived governmental acquiescence to militant means is associated with willingness to employ militant means to achieve dissimilar ends. The specific group to which the government acquiesces is less important than whether militant actions are regarded as actually having succeeded in the past.

Acquiescence, Militancy, Subjective Affective Positions,
and Ends

Perhaps the relationship between perceived acquiescence and militancy reflects a more basic relationship between dissatisfactions or ends and militancy. People who view the government as acquiescing to militancy may also be those who are most dissatisfied with their status and political power and who most strongly disapprove of the Roxbury rioting. After introducing controls for dissatisfactions and ends, the relationship between militancy and acquiescence might disappear. Yet Table 5-13 demonstrates that the relationship between acquiescence and militancy remains even after we control for dissatisfactions and ends. In all ten cases, the direction of the relationship supports the acquiescence hypothesizing: respondents who perceive the government as acquiescing to

Table 5-13. Correlations (Gamma) Between Perceived Acquiescence and Militancy, Controlling for Subjective Affective Position and Ends

| | Subjective Affective Position | | | | Ends | |
| | Status | | Political | | Riot Approval | |
	Less than deserve	Right amount & Too much	Less than deserve	Right amount & Too much	Low	Medium & High
Militancy						
Antiblack Militancy	+.63	+.43	+.38	+.52	+.59	+.44
Antigovern-mental Militancy	+.09	+.19	+.10	+.25	–	–

militant means are more militant themselves. And as was the case in the bivariate relationships between acquiescence and militancy, we once again find that perceived past acquiescence is much more strongly related than perceived future acquiescence to militancy.

Interviewed Boston white men who are dissatisfied with their status and their political power, as well as those who disapprove of the Roxbury riot, are most militant. Table 5-14 reveals that, in every case, dissatisfied and disapproving men who see the government as acquiescing to militant means are more militant than dissatisfied and disapproving men who perceive the government as resisting militant means. Satisfied and approving men who believe that militant tactics succeed are more militant than satisfied and approving men who think that militant tactics fail to win governmental concessions. Both perceived acquiescence, on the one hand, and dissatisfactions and ends, on the other hand, contribute to militancy; and each leads to greater willingness to support militant, unconventional political means.

These data demonstrate that the Marxian acquiescence hypothesizing needs partial revision. Marx implies that true radicals make utilitarian calculations about which means should be employed to achieve a particular end. Utilitarian calculations about whether militant tactics will succeed do influence Bostonians' willingness to adopt militant tactics: respondents who think that the government acquiesces to militant tactics are more likely to be militants. Yet these utilitarian calculations occur within a nonutilitarian framework: a person's ends and dissatisfactions also affect his willingness to employ militant tactics. Dissatisfied people and people who disapprove of black rioting are generally most militant; but all of the dissatisfied and all of the disapproving are not militant, and some of the satisfied and some of the approving are militant. Among the dissatisfied and the disapproving, and among the satisfied and the approving, utilitarian calculations concerning governmental acquiescence distinguishes the militants from the nonmilitants. Perceived governmental ac-

Table 5-14. Effect of Perceived Acquiescence on Militancy, Controlling for Subjective Affective Position and Ends

	Perceived Acqui-escence	Antiblack Militancy*		Antigovernmental† Militancy	
		Percent	Number	Percent	Number
Subjective Affective Status					
Less respect than deserve	High	53%	(15)	22%	(23)
	Low	18%	(11)	−††	−††
Right amount and too much respect	High	19%	(83)	10%	(138)
	Low	6%	(51)	0%	(19)
Subjective Affective Political Power (Bussing)					
Less attention than deserve	High	31%	(42)	16%	(74)
	Low	16%	(31)	−††	−††
Right amount and too much attention	High	16%	(45)	8%	(73)
	Low	0%	(23)	0%	(12)
Ends (Riot Approval)					
Low approval	High	38%	(21)	−	−
	Low	6%	(17)	−	−
Medium and high approval	High	20%	(82)	−	−
	Low	9%	(47)	−	−

* The cell figures represent the percentage of respondents in each category who said that they considered using guns against Negroes during the 1967 Roxbury riot; the numbers in parentheses indicate the total number of cases from which percentages were calculated.

† The cell figures represent the percentage of respondents in each category who were in the two highest scalar positions on the antigovernmental militancy scale; the numbers in parentheses represent the total number of cases from which the percentages were calculated.

†† Number of cases in category less than ten.

quiescence should thus be viewed as an intervening variable between dissatisfactions and ends, on the one hand, and militancy, on the other hand. Perceptions of governmental acquiescence "trigger" the dissatisfied, making those who are already most likely to be militants even more likely to take violent action against their opponents.

Objective Class and Militancy

Late 1960's white militancy was often viewed by commentators as a class phenomenon. The "hardhat" — the blue-collar worker — was popularly linked with militant white reaction to black demands. Survey data collected between 1965 and 1970 somewhat support this view. Morris and Jeffries, and Campbell and Schuman, discovered that whites with little education and low skill jobs were slightly more militant.[1][2]

In spite of these findings, three crucial questions remain. First, we know that white militancy directed at black targets is slightly more prevalent within the working class than within the middle class, but we do not really know whether militancy directed at other targets is also more prevalent within the working class. Is white antigovernmental militancy also more pronounced among blue-collar workers? Second, we now know that antiblack militancy is partially a class phenomenon, but we do not know *why* it is a class phenomenon. Does the relationship between militancy and objective class merely reflect other class related variables? Third, we do not know whether the same factors lead to white militancy in the working class and in the middle class. Is white militancy the same phenomenon among blue- and white-collar Boston men?

Is White Militancy a Class Phenomenon?

Are both antiblack and antigovernmental militancy more prevalent among blue-collar workers? An answer emerges from Tables 5-15 and 5-16. Blue-collar respondents are almost twice as likely to have considered using guns to protect themselves during the 1967 Roxbury riot (Table 5-15). But the relationship between objective class and antigovernmental militancy is similar in strength but opposite in direction (Table 5-16). While only 17% of the blue-collar respondents occupy the three highest scalar positions on the antigovernmental militancy scale, 37% of the white-collar respondents fall within these militant scalar positions.[1][3] Both antiblack and antigovernmental militancy are related to objective class, but antiblack militancy is found more often among blue-collar respondents and antigovernmental militancy is more prevalent among white-collar respondents.

Why Is Militancy a Class Phenomenon?

Why is militancy a class related phenomenon? Why does the direction of the relationship differ for antiblack and antigovernmental militancy? These questions could be answered in two ways. First, difficult to measure attitudinal differences could exist between white-collar and blue-collar respondents. If this were the case, then further analysis of the Boston data would prove useless. One might then speculate on the effect of early child-rearing practices upon a person's later militancy. The more permissive upbringing of our white-collar respondents, one might argue, leads them to feel that they can challenge parental and governmental authority without serious repercussions; hence, their greater willingness to take militant action against the government. The stricter practices of working class parents, on the other hand, would induce a fear of parental and governmental authority in blue-collar workers; their authority frustrations might then be displaced upon nongovernmental groups, such as blacks.[1][4]

Table 5-15. Objective Class and Antiblack Militancy

	Objective Class	
	Blue-Collar (N = 154)	White-Collar (N = 138)
Antiblack Militancy		
At any time during the riot did you *consider* using a gun to protect yourself or your family?		
Did *not* consider using a gun	76%	85%
Did consider using a gun	18	10
DK/NA	6	5
	100%	100%
	G = −.32*	

* D.K.'s and N.A.'s excluded in Gamma calculation.

Table 5-16. Objective Class and Antigovernmental Militancy

		Objective Class	
		Blue-Collar (N = 154)	White-Collar (N = 137)*
Antigovernmental Militancy			
Low	0	8%	7%
	1	13	10
	2	32	23
	3	30	23
	4	10	23
	5	5	12
High	6	2	2
		100%	100%
		G = +.25	

* Excludes one case omitted from scaling because of missing values.

One could also seek the reasons for the differences between blue- and white-collar militancy in measurable attitudinal factors which vary with objective class. In previous sections, we demonstrated that political and status dissatisfactions predict both antiblack and antigovernmental militancy; we also showed that a stronger relationship exists between political power dissatisfaction and antiblack militancy than between political power dissatisfaction and antigovernmental militancy. After investigating Tables 5-17 and 5-18, in which the relationships between objective class and status and political power dissatisfactions are delineated, the reason for the class differences in antiblack militancy becomes clear. While blue-collar respondents are only slightly more likely than white-collar respondents to be dissatisfied with their status (Table 5-17) they are twice as likely to be dissatisfied with their political power over city government decisions on bussing school children (Table 5-18). Since antiblack militancy is strongly related to political dissatisfactions, we can see that the relationship between antiblack militancy and lower objective class position may largely result from the prevalence of political power dissatisfaction among blue-collar respondents.

Further evidence of substantial political power dissatisfaction among our blue-collar respondents emerges from Figure 5-5, in which objective class is related to the difference between the person's own rung on the status and political power ladders and the rungs which he assigned to blacks on each ladder. As was pointed out earlier, these differences represent cognitive status and political power relative deprivation, with blacks as the comparative reference group. As with status dissatisfactions, we find little difference between working and middle class respondents in the extent to which they are the victims of subjective cognitive status relative deprivation; 17% of the blue-collar respondents, and 12% of the white-collar respondents, feel that they have less status than blacks. Yet when we turn to political power relative deprivation, large objective class differences emerge. Fully 70% of the blue-collar respondents classify themselves at least four rungs lower than blacks on bussing political power, yet only 38% of the white-collar respondents manifested similarly extreme political power relative deprivation. While almost 90% of the interviewed blue-collar men maintain that they have less political power than blacks, only 70% of the white-collar men responded in this disaffected fashion.[15]

A similar explanation arises from examining Table 5-19, in which objective class is related to approval of the 1967 riot (ends). As with political power dissatisfaction, we find that riot approval is strongly related to objective class: blue-collar respondents are twice as likely to disapprove of the Roxbury riot.[16] Our earlier explanation is applicable here too: the relationship between antiblack militancy and objective class results from the preponderance of riot disapproval within the blue-collar group.

Table 5-17. Objective Class and Subjective Affective Status

	Objective Class	
	Blue-Collar (N = 154)	White-Collar (N = 138)
Subjective Affective Status		
Would you say that people like yourself get:		
Less respect than you deserve	15%	13%
Just about the right amount of respect/ and more respect than you deserve	82	80
DK/NA	3	7
	100%	100%
	G = +.05*	

* D.K.'s and N.A.'s excluded in Gamma calculation.

Table 5-18. Objective Class and Subjective Affective Political Power (Bussing)

	Objective Class	
	Blue-Collar (N = 154)	White-Collar (N = 138)
Subjective Affective Political Power (Bussing)		
In making decisions about school bussing, would you say city officials pay:		
Less attention [than deserved to people like yourself]	53%	28%
Just about the right amount of attention/and more attention than deserved to people like yourself	27	57
DK/NA	19	14
	99%*	99%*
	G = +.60†	

* Deviation from 100% due to rounding.

† D.K.'s and N.A.'s excluded in Gamma calculation.

Figure 5-5 Objective Class and Cognitive Status and Political Power (Bussing) Relative Deprivation.

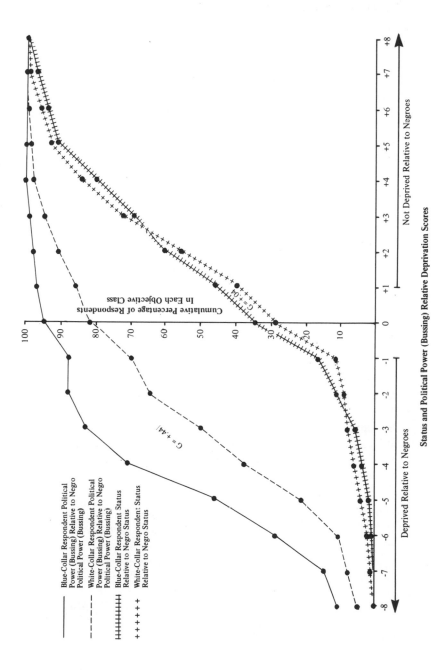

Table 5-19. Objective Class and Ends

	Objective Class	
	Blue-Collar (N = 154)	White-Collar (N = 138)
Ends		
Do you think that the people in Roxbury:		
Should have waited patiently for the government to do something to help them	25%	12%
Should . . . have used other tactics to protest in a more peaceful way	67	70
Were justified in rioting	3	12
DK/NA	6	5
	101%*	99%*
	G = +.47†	

* Deviation from 100% due to rounding.

† D.K.'s and N.A.'s excluded in Gamma calculation.

Do the Same Factors Lead to Militancy in Both Blue-Collar and White-Collar Groups?

An important question remains: Do blue-collar militancy and white-collar militancy result from the same factors? Table 5-20 details the intra-objective class correlations between dissatisfactions, ends, and militancy. Even after controlling for objective class, the correlations remain consistent in direction and

Table 5-20. Correlations (Gamma) Between Subjective Affective Positions, Ends, and Militancy, Controlling for Objective Class

	Objective Class					
	Blue-Collar			White-Collar		
	Status	Political (Bussing)	Ends	Status	Political (Bussing)	Ends
Militancy						
Antiblack Militancy	−.30	−.26	−.24	−.52	−.27	−.44
Antigovernmental Militancy	−.21	−.20	−	−.51	−.10	−

(with one exception) moderate or strong. Among both blue- and white-collar respondents, status dissatisfaction, political dissatisfaction, and riot disapproval result in greater militancy. As in the earlier data on dissatisfactions and militancy, we find that status dissatisfactions predict militancy better than political power dissatisfactions, and that a stronger correlation exists between political power dissatisfaction and antiblack militancy than between political power dissatisfaction and antigovernmental militancy.

Table 5-21. Correlations (Gamma) Between Perceived Acquiescence and Militancy, Controlling for Objective Class

| | Objective Class | |
	Blue-Collar	White-Collar
Militancy		
Antiblack Militancy	+.37	+.78
Antigovernmental Militancy	+.10	+.18

Table 5-21 sets forth the intra-objective class correlations between perceived governmental acquiescence and militancy. These correlations are identical in direction and somewhat similar in strength to the uncontrolled relationships discussed earlier. Once again, larger correlations exist between perceived past acquiescence and antiblack militancy than between perceived future acquiescence and antigovernmental militancy.

The relationships between militancy and its attitudinal correlates are similar for both blue- and white-collar groups. The same factors predict blue-collar militancy and white-collar militancy: political dissatisfactions, status dissatisfactions, riot disapproval, and perceived governmental acquiescence. But one problem remains unresolved: we have not yet uncovered any factor which could explain the greater antigovernmental militancy among white-collar respondents.

A possible explanation lies in Seymour Martin Lipset's writings. The more authoritarian blue-collar respondents, Lipset might reason, will not militantly challenge governmental authority, but will attack other groups, such as blacks, who threaten their political power and status. Gus Tyler, assistant president of the ILGWU, thus points out that:

Since our worker does not know how to deal with the system, he tries to do the next best thing: to act within the system to protect his own skin. And in our torn and turbulent cities, it is too often his "skin" that determines his mood.[17]

The less authoritarian white-collar respondents, however, might not fear challenging governmental authority, and might be less likely to displace their dissatisfactions onto other groups.

During the past decade, criticism of Lipset's authoritarianism argument has steadily increased. These critiques have proceeded on two levels. First, secondary analyses of survey data have shed doubt on Lipset's reasoning.[18] Lipsitz has shown that authoritarianism is largely a function of education; after controlling for education, blue-collar workers are no more authoritarian than white-collar workers.[19] Working class authoritarianism thus results not from any innate class characteristics, but rather from the lower educational level of the working class. Hamilton demonstrates that northern white working class respondents are no more conservative on racial issues than northern middle class respondents.[20]

Criticisms of the Lipset authoritarianism theorizing have also occurred on a second level. Even if we accept Lipset's data as accurately reflecting differences between the working and middle classes, we can nonetheless devise other explanations which are equally as convincing as the authoritarianism speculation.[21] This search for alternate explanations provides the context for our reasoning concerning the higher antigovernmental militancy among our white-collar respondents. Blue-collar respondents are substantially more likely than white-collar respondents to be dissatisfied with their political power. We can speculate that blue-collar respondents are more likely to view the government as an omnipotent force which neither provides for their needs nor yields to the demands made by disadvantaged whites. White-collar respondents are more likely to be satisfied with their political power. Seeing themselves as actually exerting influence over governmental decision-making, the government appears to them as neither omnipotent nor uninfluenceable. Since the government acquiesces to popular demands, white-collar respondents would be more likely to feel that antigovernmental militancy is not futile. Blue-collar respondents, possibly perceiving the government as more omnipotent and more totalitarian, would be afraid of taking antigovernmental militant actions and more likely to believe that militancy would be met with harsh repressive measures.

Support for this reasoning emerges from Tables 5-22 and 5-23, which display the relationships between objective class and perceived governmental acquiescence. While white-collar respondents are only slightly more likely to believe that Roxbury has received "a lot more help" since the 1967 riots, they are substantially more likely to feel that the Mayor, faced with a sit-in at City Hall to protest the dangerous school-crossing, would "try to do something about the protestors' demands." Many white-collar respondents view local government as relatively benevolent, but many blue-collar respondents see the government as less benevolent and more likely to take repressive action against protestors.

The Boston survey data reveal limitations in Marx's theorizing and in our Marxian-Weberian theoretical scheme. Neither theoretical scheme can stand unrevised. In the final chapter, the Boston data will be employed to modify both theoretical frameworks.

Table 5-22. Objective Class and Perceived Acquiescence to Black Rioters

	Objective Class	
	Blue-Collar (N = 154)	White-Collar (N = 138)
Perceived Acquiescence to Black Rioters		
In the summer of 1967 there was a Negro riot in Roxbury. Do you think:		
[Roxbury gets] about the same help now as [it] did before	26%	17%
[Roxbury gets] a little more help [now]	23	31
Roxbury has gotten a lot more help from the government since the riot	35	39
DK/NA	16	13
	100%	100%
	G = +.14*	

* D.K.'s and N.A.'s excluded in Gamma calculation.

Table 5-23. Objective Class and Perceived Acquiescence to Antigovernmental Protestors

	Objective Class	
	Blue-Collar (N = 154)	White-Collar (N = 138)
Perceived Acquiescence to Anti-governmental Protestors		
What do you think the Mayor would do if a sit-in protesting the school crossing were staged at City Hall? Do you think he would:		
Order the people arrested	7%	7%
Try to ignore them	34	18
Try to do something about their demands	46	66
DK/NA	13	9
	100%	100%
	G = +.33*	

* D.K.'s and N.A.'s excluded in Gamma calculation

6 Conclusions

I find myself surrounded by miseries I can no longer cope with. So I want to try a vaster, more encompassing remedy. I would have preferred a collective analysis, but since that is not possible, let us try Marxism. [1]

Anais Nin

Introduction

"The Americans are worlds behind in all theoretical things. . . ." [2] So wrote Engels to Sorge in 1886. Engels' nineteenth century criticism of American socialists represents an apt description of much contemporary American political science. American political scientists have not provided theoretical interpretations of 1960's and 1970's white militancy. Empirical investigations of white militancy were conducted, but these surveys were largely unguided by theoretical concerns. The failure to incorporate middle-level theory into survey research introduced biases into findings. Many research questions were neither considered nor posed. The causes of black militancy were sought in black dissatisfactions with the American socio-political structure; but only minimal attention was directed at white dissatisfactions with the structure of American society and politics as the motive force behind white militancy. Given the absence within academe of alternative explanations for white militancy, popular commentators seized upon a plausible yet pernicious explanation: white militancy arises from the racist, antiblack sentiments of individual whites. Rather than eagerly adopting a critical stance through thoroughly searching for alternate explanations of white militancy, established social science apparently accepted the conventional wisdom. As all of us should have realized long before, social scientists are not too different from other Americans: given a logical and widely believed explanation of a contemporary phenomenon such as white militancy, we too will accede to the explanation — and unknowingly bias our studies toward supporting the current conventional wisdom.

Political scientists' atheoretical approach and their failure to test fully the conventional wisdom could conceivably have had no effect upon survey results. If popular explanations had proved to have substantial validity, then my criticism of these surveys could easily be relegated to an interesting academic speculative footnote. Yet survey researchers had terrific difficulty in uncovering adequate attitudinal correlates of white militancy. The atheoretical approach bore few enticing fruit. The empirical findings of these surveys were largely negative: we discovered many attitudinal variables which were unrelated to white militancy, and only few which were related to it.[3]

Adopting a more theoretical approach might have had only aesthetic advantages. The negative findings of the surveys could have lent preliminary evidence for the need to revise various theories of political action. But the Boston survey demonstrates that adopting a theoretical stance in studying white militancy has both practical and aesthetic advantages. Militancy among Boston white men is moderately related to several theoretically significant attitudes. Some of the motives lying behind white militancy were found in attitudes which had not been tapped in previous studies. Those respondents who are dissatisfied with their political power over bussing decisions, those who feel that they are accorded less status than they deserve, and those who believe that the city government acquiesces to militant protest activities are most militant. Some of the hunches promulgated by the conventional wisdom also find support in the Boston data: blue-collar respondents are most likely to support militant actions directed against the black community. But some whites holding white-collar jobs are also likely to take militant actions; and white-collar respondents are most likely militantly to oppose the government.

Theorizing and empirical investigation cannot proceed in isolation from each other. Jerzy Wiatr, a Polish sociologist, points out that ". . . the relationship between ideology and science in sociology has to be seen dialectically, not as a relationship of different forms of thinking, but as the relationship of different aspects of the same thinking about reality."[4] The same can be said for the relationship between theory and survey research in political science. Theorizing and survey research are not different endeavors, but integrally related aspects of the same endeavor. Just as theorizing without empirical examination of hypotheses is incomplete, so survey research unguided by theoretical concerns possesses only limited utility.

The purpose of explicitly recognizing the relationship between theorizing and empirical research is not limited to posing novel research questions or revealing implicit research biases. An explicit recognition of the bond between theory and research allows both theory and research to fulfill complementary functions: theory being continually revised in the light of new research findings, and research questions being continually reformulated in the light of new theoretical explanations. The revision of theorizing is the final task of this study. The task is threefold. First, Marx's theorizing on the relationship between the objective class structure, subjective class consciousness, and political action must be revised. Second, hypotheses derived from our Marxian-Weberian theoretical scheme, delineated in Chapter 3, must be restated. And third, the use of middle-level theory in survey research must be reconsidered.

Revising Marx's Perspective

*Objective Class Structure and Subjective Class
Consciousness*

In Marx's eyes, the objective class structure forms a continuum; rather than two classes separated by a wide economic gulf, a multiplicity of class groupings exists. Polarization differentiates objective classes from each other, but this is a polarization of subjective class consciousness, and not a structural polarization. According to Marx, workers perceive a large relative gap between themselves and those at the top of the objective class structure, but most middle class members perceive no such gap.

A fault was identified in Marx's theorizing on the objective class structure and subjective class consciousness. Marx implies that the individual's status, economic position, and political power are perfectly correlated with each other. Since they are perfectly correlated, Marx makes no conceptual or empirical attempt to distinguish among them.

The findings derived from the Boston survey suggest that a threefold revision of this part of Marx's theorizing may be necessary. Revisions are needed in Marx's hypothesizing on the relationships among economic position, status, and political power; in his theorizing on the attitudinal polarization between the working and middle classes; and in his conception of the revolutionary role of the proletariat. First, the data reveal that self-perceptions of economic position, status, and political power are not perfectly correlated with each other. A person can believe that he possesses great status but only limited political power. Weber was correct: class, status, and political power are both conceptually and empirically distinct stratification dimensions. Contrary to Marx's theorizing, perceived economic position is no more strongly related to perceived political power than is perceived status to perceived political power.

In discussing classes in different countries, Marx emphasizes the effects of dissimilar historical and environmental circumstances upon class development and the growth of subjective class consciousness.[5] Despite Marx's sensitivity to the peculiar circumstances of individual countries, he fails to consider fully either the effect of national ideology upon subjective class consciousness, or the revolutionary potential of subjective class consciousness which is not solely economic in nature.

Marx criticizes middle class revolutions, such as the American Revolution of 1776, for fostering the notion that political emancipation represents the end-all of revolution. Political emancipation is crucial, but it constitutes only a necessary first step toward the more basic human emancipation which will result from abolishing the division of labor. Marx seems to think that middle class revolutions will succeed in their own terms: political emancipation will be achieved, and as a result, workers will either be economically dissatisfied or they will not be dissatisfied at all.

In *The Communist Manifesto,* Marx and Engels write that "what the bourgeoisie therefore produces, above all, are its own grave-diggers."[6] In writing this, Marx and Engels were specifically referring to the internal contradictions of the capitalist economic system: the necessity for larger workshops will reduce the number of capitalists, and will eventually lead to the working class revolution. But as Lukacs indicates, Marx's point ". . . is valid ideologically as well as economically."[7] The American middle class revolution fomented an ideology in which both status and political equality were held to be realities of the new nation's socio-political structure. The United States has failed to make the reality meet the ideology: some Boston respondents see themselves as possessing less status and political power than they should. Because of the importance of status equality in the Americanism ideology, perceived status inequalities may assume a more important role than perceived economic inequalities in determining political views and political action.

Marxian thinkers have long assumed that status discontents are counter-revolutionary. Lukacs thus asserts that "status-consciousness — a real historical factor — masks class consciousness; in fact it prevents it from emerging at all."[8] However, in a country in which an ideology of status equality is widely accepted, the lack of status equality might provide a revolutionary force. Those who have less status than others may blame the socio-political structure for failing to insure status equality. If the socio-political structure fails to meet its own criterion of success, then those who are dissatisfied with their status might believe that the structure must be changed. Not only might status dissatisfactions prove to be a revolutionary force, but such dissatisfactions might not impede the growth of economic dissatisfactions and class consciousness. The individual who faults the socio-political structure for its inability to produce status equality might generalize his dissatisfactions. Status dissatisfactions might thus grow into class dissatisfactions.

The Boston data also indicate that a second revision in Marx's theorizing on the objective class structure and subjective class consciousness is necessary. Marx maintains that the all-important differentiation between the working and middle classes lies not in a wide economic gap, but in greatly differing attitudes toward the socio-political structure. The Boston survey reveals that some attitudinal polarization does exist between Boston white men with blue-collar occupations and those with white-collar occupations. However, this polarization is neither great nor of uniform magnitude in all attitudes toward the socio-political structure. Little difference exists between blue- and white-collar respondents' attitudes towards their own status; approximately 15% of both groups maintain that they receive less respect than they should. However, more blue-collar respondents are dissatisfied with their political power over Boston city government decisions on school bussing than are white-collar respondents. As Pete Hamill says, "the working-class white man sees injustice and politicking everywhere in this town now, with himself in the role of victim."[9]

Marx's works do not provide an adequate explanation for this finding. Following Marx's reasoning, we would have hypothesized that blue-collar respondents would be more dissatisfied with both their status and their political power than white-collar respondents. Yet this is not true of our 1970 Boston respondents. Why are blue-collar respondents substantially more dissatisfied with their political power than white-collar respondents, but no more dissatisfied with their status?

The reason for this may lie in the groups which blue- and white-collar respondents compare themselves with when they think of their status and political power. School bussing is a race-related issue; the interviewed Bostonians believe that blacks have more influence on city government decisions on school bussing than any other group. When Boston whites think of their power over school bussing decisions, they probably compare their own power to the power which they imagine is wielded by blacks. In contemplating status, however, no one group is singled out as the sole important referent.[10]

The Boston white who is dissatisfied with his status might justify the greater respect accorded to other groups by pointing to either inadequacies within the American socio-political structure, or by comparing his own relatively low status to the respect accorded to high status groups, such as doctors and the wealthy. But the Boston white who is dissatisfied with his political power would compare his own political power to that wielded by blacks. The perception that a low status group is wielding great influence over city government decisions on an issue as important as school bussing might be particularly galling to those whites whose status and economic standing are most similar to the black community. In a similar vein, Pettigrew asserts that "relative deprivation for the white working-class Wallace supporters in Gary . . . derives largely from perceiving that groups regarded as lower in status and skills — especially black Americans — are unfairly gaining on their position."[11] The white-collar worker, even if he perceives blacks as having substantial influence over school bussing decisions, could at least take refuge in his own higher status. The blue-collar worker, accorded less status, has no such refuge, and thus might be more dissatisfied with the greater political power of a group with status similar to his own.

Marx, in speculating on subjective class consciousness, should have realized that attitudinal polarization might be substantially more evident on some issues than others. In defining subjective class consciousness, he should have explicitly considered the importance not only of the perception of a relative gap between workers and those at the top of the class structure, but also of the specific group which is regarded as being at the top. The nature of that reference group might determine the target of the action flowing from subjective class consciousness.

A third revision in Marx's theorizing on the objective class structure and subjective class consciousness is also suggested by the Boston data. Marx asserts that the proletariat, as the only class whose dissatisfactions can be mediated through a total overthrow of the capitalist system, is the truly revolutionary class. But Marx maintains that economic dissatisfactions provide the sole revolutionary impetus for this class. Political and status dissatisfactions are not revolutionary forces, for neither have objective class bases.

The Boston study reveals that status dissatisfactions may not be class based. Some scholars might maintain that these data indicate the "bourgeoisification" of the working class: as working class incomes increase, the working class becomes more like the conservative middle class. Yet an alternate explanation is equally plausible. As Robert Nisbet maintains, the American middle class has become increasingly radical.[12] The absence of objective class based status dissatisfactions in our 1970 Boston sample could be viewed not as evidence of the lack of radicalism within the working class, but as evidence of the common revolutionary interests of the working and middle classes.

These common interests, however, are limited. Data discussed in the preceding chapter indicate that political dissatisfactions are more prevalent within the working class, and that working class members are most likely to believe that the government will take harsh action to quell dissent. While revolutionary action stemming from status dissatisfaction is equally likely to arise from the middle as from the working class, revolutionary action stemming from political dissatisfactions might have a working class base.[13]

Marx asserts that economic dissatisfactions will be a major factor differentiating the working class from the middle class, and that economic dissatisfactions will unify working class members into a cohesive political force. Yet study after study demonstrates that blue-collar workers are the most politically discontented group: they are most likely to believe that voting makes little difference and that political power is concentrated in the hands of the wealthy. Rather than ignoring such dissatisfactions through repeating the Marxist catechism that all political issues are based in economics and that economic dissatisfactions provide the sole unifying factor within the working class, Marxian theorists would do well to reconsider the revolutionary potential of political power issues within advanced capitalist societies.

Marx accepts the possibility that the real wages of the working class will increase and that the working class standard of living will improve. However, he stresses that working class wages and standards of living will always remain substantially lower than those of the middle class. But perhaps relative economic deprivations are not always as important as Marx believed. If working class wages and standards of living have been raised to a high level relative to those of ten, twenty, or thirty years ago, then economic dissatisfactions might decrease — even if the relative gap between the proletariat and the middle class has not grown smaller. If economic dissatisfactions do decrease when a certain standard of living has been attained, then we must search for other class based dissatisfactions which do not decrease with economic improvement. And political power dissatisfactions may provide just such a class based revolutionary impetus which will remain even after economic dissatisfactions have lessened.[14]

Political Action

In theorizing on subjective class consciousness and political action, Marx fails to distinguish adequately between the effect of knowledge on action, and the effect of dissatisfactions on action. Marx implies that the person who is aware of a large relative gap between himself and those at the top of the objective class structure will inevitably be dissatisfied with that gap. Conceptually, the blurring of knowledge and dissatisfactions leads to oversimplification: a person can be aware of his relatively low position in the objective class structure without being dissatisfied with that position. Although the white Boston respondent who perceives himself as possessing low status and little political power is also likely to hold status and political power dissatisfactions, the relationship is far from perfect. Further, the effect of perceived status, class, and political power positions on militancy differs from the effect of dissatisfactions with those positions on militancy. Self-perceptions of status, political power, and economic positions are inconsistently weakly correlated with militancy; status and political power dissatisfactions are consistently moderately correlated with militancy. In searching for the motives behind militancy in particular and revolutionary action in general, we should not assume that knowledge of one's disadvantaged position in society is sufficient to lead to action. Rather, dissatisfactions with that position provide the key motive force.

Marx's assumption of the total overlap between economic class, status, and political power clouds his theorizing on the relationship between subjective class consciousness and political action. Status discontents are more strongly related to both antiblack and antigovernmental militancy than are political discontents. These data from the Boston survey reveal that two changes should be made in this aspect of Marxian theory. First, national ideology as a potential revolutionary force should be given a place in Marxian theorizing. Because of the emphasis upon status equality in the Americanism ideology, the perceived lack of such equality becomes highly salient to many of the interviewed Boston whites. Economic inequality is tolerated as an acceptable although distasteful ingredient of the socio-political structure, but status inequality can be regarded principally as indicating the failure of the American socio-political structure.[15] Further, attempts at redressing status inequality are likely to be made through militant political action.

A second and complementary adjustment must also be made in this aspect of Marxian theory: a clear distinction should be drawn between structural and other sorts of discontents. In addition to the importance of status in the Americanism ideology, another reason for the greater importance of status than political discontents as a determinant of militancy may lie in the possibility that status discontents are essentially discontents with the socio-political structure. However, political discontents may be centered on other groups within that structure. Structural discontents — whether specifically status, economic, or political — are more likely than nonstructural discontents to lead to revolutionary action.

In Marxian theorizing, the individual's choice of militant or pacific means will not be determined by whether he is satisfied or dissatisfied, or by whether he is a radical or a conservative, but by his calculations of which means are most likely to succeed. The true radical, in Marx's mind, will make purely utilitarian calculations concerning which means should be employed to achieve a particular end. The white Bostonians interviewed in 1970 do not fully meet Marx's criteria for true radicalism; however, Marx's theorizing is partially borne out by the data. Respondents who are most dissatisfied with their status or political power and who have the most extreme ends are more likely to be militants. Yet perceptions of governmental acquiescence also affect militancy. Among both the satisfied and the dissatisfied, those who think that the government will acquiesce to militant tactics are more likely to be militants than those who believe that the government will not acquiesce to militant tactics.

Marx's assumption of utilitarian calculations provides a partially accurate picture of the genesis of militant attitudes. However, these utilitarian calculations occur within a nonutilitarian framework. The basic cause of white militancy lies in status and political power dissatisfactions. Acquiescence acts as an intervening variable between dissatisfactions and militancy, making those who are already predisposed toward militancy even more likely to take militant actions.

Revising the Marxian-Weberian Theoretical Scheme

If empirical research is to contribute to the growth of middle-level theory, then theorizing must be revised after it has been subjected to empirical examination. The outcome of empirical studies should not only be discussions of which hypotheses are supported by the data and which are not, but also a discussion of new areas of hypothesizing which can then be expanded upon by other researchers.

The Boston survey data indicate areas of strength and weakness in our Marxian-Weberian theoretical scheme. The areas of strength lie in the definition of the independent variables and the conceptual differentiation among those variables; the areas of weakness lie in the hypothesized relationships between the independent variables and militancy. The data discussed in the preceding chapter indicate that economic class, status, and political power are perceived as different stratification dimensions by most of the 301 Boston respondents. When ranking themselves and other groups on these dimensions, we find that individuals or groups accorded a low rank on one dimension are not necessarily given comparably low ranks on the other dimensions. Class, status, and political power are regarded as distinct by the respondents; political scientists would do well to retain these distinctions in their future survey research.

In our Marxian-Weberian theoretical scheme, political power was conceptualized as consisting of numerous internal hierarchies. These internal hierarchies are specific to both particular issues and different levels of government. A person could feel that he exerts influence over local but not over federal governmental decisions. The importance of this conceptual differentiation within the political power dimension is demonstrated by the Boston data. We find that those people who believe themselves to have little general political power do not necessarily who believe themselves to have little general political power do not necessarily also feel that they have little political power on a specific issue — city government decisions on school bussing.

Our surprising finding that many Boston whites feel powerless over city government decisions on school bussing also indicates the importance of conceptually differentiating within the political power dimension. Boston's School Committee has catered to the wishes of the white majority in resisting state and federal demands for ending de facto segregation in the public schools. Yet tremendous pressure has been put on Boston by both state and federal governments: desegregate now or no more education funds will be forthcoming. In asserting that they have little power over city government decisions on school bussing, our white Boston respondents may be acknowledging their fatalism about city government's ability to influence the course of local education. Boston whites may feel that the school bussing issue will be settled on the state or federal level. Despite the Boston government's resistance to state and federal demands for desegregation, white Bostonians still may believe that they have little control over bussing decisions — for they may think that these decisions will not be made at the local governmental level.

While theorizing on economic class, status, and political power, we emphasized the need to distinguish the individual's objective position on each dimension from his perception of that position (subjective cognitive level); we also maintained that perceived economic, status, and political power positions should be distinguished from dissatisfactions with those positions (subjective affective level). Previous researchers dealing with class consciousness and political action often blurred these distinctions.[16] The Boston data support the argument for conceptually and empirically distinguishing perceived position from dissatisfaction. Perceived position is not perfectly correlated with dissatisfaction; and when each is correlated with militancy, dissatisfactions emerge as a more powerful and consistent predictor than perceived position. The key element in class consciousness is thus not whether people believe their economic position, status, or political power to be high or low, but whether they are satisfied or dissatisfied with those positions.

Although the Boston survey reveals that our Marxian-Weberian theoretical scheme provides a useful framework for analyzing perceived status, economic standing, and political power, the data also indicate that the framework proves inadequate in predicting militancy. The principal hypothesis developed in our Marxian-Weberian theoretical scheme centered on the independence of ends and means. We speculated that a person's choice of ends is determined by his actual status, economic position, and political power; by his cognitive perceptions of his status, economic standing, and political power; and by his dissatisfactions with his status, economic standing, and political power. On the other hand, we also hypothesized that these factors exert no influence on a person's choice of means. Both the right radical and the left radical will choose means to accomplish their ends only after they have decided which means are most likely to succeed; the means that will be chosen are those which have been judged most likely to influence the government.

The Boston data fail to support this hypothesizing. Means and ends are not independent of each other. Status and political power dissatisfactions — factors which were hypothesized as influencing a person's choice of ends — also affect his choice of means. Yet the data do suggest that ends and means are chosen in different ways. The individual who is dissatisfied with his status or political power, we can speculate, will be most likely to choose extreme ends. Dissatisfactions also lead to a willingness to use militant means. But dissatisfactions alone do not always cause an individual to become a militant. Coupled with dissatisfactions, we must also look at whether the individual believes that the government will acquiesce to militant action. Perceived governmental acquiescence thus should be viewed as a theoretically crucial intervening variable — the triggering mechanism — between dissatisfaction and militancy.

Survey Research and Middle-Level Theory

Value-free research is neither possible nor desirable. It is not possible because all people — including social scientists — consciously and unconsciously treasure certain values. These values determine our perception of political reality. A social scientist with liberal values will view political reality in one way and will ask certain questions in his attempts to understand political reality better. A social scientist with conservative values will view political reality in another way and will ask other questions. The values held by the researcher shape the questions he asks.

Value-free research is not desirable because the understanding of political reality arrived at by social scientists inevitably feeds back into and affects the political perceptions and political decisions of those who are not social scientists. The Kerner Commission, in blaming white racism for the black riots of the 1960's, affected both the governmental response and the white reactions to the riots. If the Kerner Commission had focused attention not on individual white racism but on the status, economic, and political inequalities which affect both whites and blacks, the governmental response and white reaction to the riots might have been different.[17] Since social science does affect political decisions, those of us who conduct social science research should make sure that our research questions allow the possibility of findings which will help us to effect our values. The research questions chosen should explicitly depend upon the values held by the researcher.

Yet objective research — research that is verifiable and replicable — is both possible and necessary. Objectivity involves not so much the choice or framing of research questions, but the methods used to answer those questions. Given a research question stated in a particular manner, the methods employed should not exclude any particular answer to that question.

The use of comprehensive middle-level theory in survey research will help us directly to address problems of values and biases in our studies. Middle-level theory will help us to confront our own values and assumptions. Through making these values and assumptions explicit, as Gunnar Myrdal and Alvin Gouldner point out, we can remove the biases introduced into our research by implicit and unacknowledged values.[18] Middle-level theory will also help us to frame better research questions. Rather than inadvertently accepting and studying those questions implied by currently popular interpretations of a particular phenomenon, middle-level theory will lead us to ask other questions as well.

The Boston survey illustrates the need for employing middle-level theory in survey research. Many popular commentators would have us believe that white militancy was based on white racism. Other possible motives lying behind white militancy were infrequently considered. Through the use of middle-level theory, we derived alternate explanations for white militancy. The plausibility of these explanations was then examined through reviewing the results of the Boston survey. We discovered that racism alone cannot account for militancy. Like much of the black community, many of our white respondents keenly feel their own lack of status and political power. As with blacks, such dissatisfactions lie behind the militancy of the white Boston men interviewed. White militancy is thus largely a misnomer. Both "white" and "black" militancy derive from similar sources: status, political, and economic inequalities in today's United States.

Appendix A
Sampling and Interviewing

The sample, designed in conjunction with Independent Research Associates, was based upon a multi-stage random cluster sampling process. Sixty sample points were randomly selected from the 1969 Boston police list, a compendium listing all Boston households and the occupations of adult household members. As was indicated in Chapter 4, the design of the sample was dictated by the joint desire to maximize the number of militant respondents, and to obtain a sample which would permit analysis of the effect of objective class placement on militancy and on the relationship between militancy and powerlessness. Research by Campbell and Schuman, and by Morris and Jeffries, had shown that support for the use of militant means is considerably greater among white males than among white females; while 8% of white males in the Campbell and Schuman sample endorse counter-rioting against blacks, only 3 % of white females gave similar responses.[1] Because of the substantially greater militancy among males, only adult white males were included in the sample. In order to permit analysis of the effect of objective class placement on militancy and on the interaction between militancy and powerlessness, the sixty sample points were divided into three groups: those sample points in which 75% of the males hold white-collar jobs, those in which 75% of the males hold blue-collar jobs, and a residual group in which occupations were mixed. The final sampling frame was equally divided between twenty-five white-collar sample points and twenty-five blue-collar sample points. Six respondents, randomly selected from the police list page corresponding to the sample point, were to be interviewed at each sample point.

I had initially planned on basing the sample on the Boston census. Four predominantly white census tracts were to be chosen: one white-collar and one blue-collar adjacent to black tracts, and one white-collar and one blue-collar not adjacent to black tracts. Due to the high residential mobility among Boston respondents and the massive urban renewal which occurred since 1960, the 1960 census was hopelessly outdated at the time this research was conducted. Use of the 1970 census would have been highly preferable to the use of the 1969 police lists, which proved to be an inadequate source. Use of the census would have permitted full identification of the demographic characteristics of the population in each census tract, and would have permitted better identification of black areas to be excluded from the frame. As in research by David W. Abbott, Louis H. Gold, and Edward T. Rogowsky, which employed a similar big city official list of residents as the sampling source, we found the police list to be greatly inaccurate.[2] Forty-three percent of the initial respondents drawn from the police list were no longer at the address recorded in the police list (or had never been at that address), and substitutes were randomly selected from the same sample point. Five sample points were discarded because they contained a high proportion of blacks, and were replaced with alternate sample points.

The desire to obtain a sample including a relatively high proportion of militants, and allowing analysis of the effects of objective class placement on militancy, obviated, for reasons of cost and practicality, the use of a sampling process which would yield respondents statistically representative of the entire Boston populace. In deciding against such a sample, we followed Eysenck's well-taken suggestion:

'the type of sample which is taken must depend on the purpose of the analysis'; hence the need for what the present writer has called 'analytic sampling'. If the purpose of an investigation is the determination of the percentage of persons within a given population holding a certain view, then obviously some form of representative sampling is called for. But when . . . the main purpose of the investigation is the comparison of persons in different social classes, then clearly the most efficient technique would be one which equalized numbers in all the groups to be compared. . . . This point should be too obvious to make, were it not for the fact that countless workers are so hypnotized by the stress commonly laid on 'representative sampling' that they forget that sampling of any kind is done for a purpose, and does not, like the Kingdom of God, carry its own salvation. It should also be noted that only by some such analysis of variable design as this will we be able to study the effects of 'interaction' between the variables included in the experiments.[3]

The analytic sample chosen allows the investigation of interaction among key variables, the modification of theoretically important hypotheses and of the theories lying behind those hypotheses, and identification of which of those hypotheses merit further research.

Interviewing urban males, and particularly blue-collar urban males, presents problems. Many of them frequently work overtime hours, and others hold two jobs; 33% of the respondents in the sample work more than forty hours each week. In an attempt to minimize the number of replacements required for the primary respondents, most interviewing was conducted at night or on weekends by trained professional interviewers; interviewers were instructed to make three call-backs. Despite this precaution, 41% of primary respondents or their replacements refused to allow the interviewer to conduct the interview, or were not at home; refusals and not-at-homes were replaced with other respondents randomly selected from the same sample point. The completion rate is similar to the urban white completion rates attained in similar studies by Abbott, Gold, and Rogowsky, and by Campbell and Schuman.[4]

Interviews were conducted in the homes of the respondents. The interview schedule was long and complex: most interviews lasted between fifty and ninety minutes. The interviews began with questions concerning 1968 presidential voting choice and party affiliation; more sensitive demographic questions concerning occupation, income, and so forth, were not asked until the conclusion of the interview. Open-end questions were always asked before close-end questions dealing with the same subject. Finally, questions concerning the major dependent variable — militancy — were covered in the latter part of the interviewing session.

Appendix B
Respondent Occupations

White-Collar Respondents

Accountants	4
Architects	1
Computer specialists	2
Trained engineers	7
Lawyers	2
Librarians	1
Chemists	1
Pharmacists	1
Health technologists and technicians	3
Religious workers	1
Social and recreation workers	2
Teachers	6
Writers, artists, entertainers	10
Managers and administrators	21
Sales workers	21
Clerical and kindred workers	39
Self-employed small businessmen	8
Part-time students	5
Other White-Collar	3
Total White-Collar Respondents	138

Blue-Collar Respondents

Building engineers	5
Craftsmen and kindred workers	62
Machine operatives	21
Transport equipment operatives	19
Laborers	24
Service workers	23
Total Blue-Collar Respondents	154

Occupation Not Ascertained

Total Not Ascertained	9
Total Respondents	301

Appendix C
Interview Schedule Questions

Subjective Cognitive Powerlessness

Status

Q. 15: Now, I'd like to go back to something we were talking about earlier – the respect given to certain groups or types of people in the United States today. (HAND YELLOW LADDER CARD) Let's say that the top of this ladder – number 9 – represents those groups of people who are given the most respect, and the bottom of the ladder – number 1 – represents those given the least respect. On what rung of the ladder would you place the types of people listed on this card? (HAND PINK GROUP CARD) Where would you place _____
_____ on the ladder? (READ OUT EACH GROUP AND RECORD ONE ANSWER FOR EACH GROUP BELOW)

Group of people	Respect		Don't Know	Refuse
	(Least)	(Most)		
Union members	32-1 -2 -3 -4 -5 -6 -7 -8 -9 -0		-X	(I)
Italians	33-1 -2 -3 -4 -5 -6 -7 -8 -9 -0		-X	(I)
Medical doctors	34-1 -2 -3 -4 -5 -6 -7 -8 -9 -0		-X	(I)
Negroes	35-1 -2 -3 -4 -5 -6 -7 -8 -9 -0		-X	(I)
Irish	36-1 -2 -3 -4 -5 -6 -7 -8 -9 -0		-X	(I)
Rich people	37-1 -2 -3 -4 -5 -6 -7 -8 -9 -0		-X	(I)
Salesmen in a department store	38-1 -2 -3 -4 -5 -6 -7 -8 -9 -0		-X	(I)
People on welfare	39-1 -2 -3 -4 -5 -6 -7 -8 -9 -0		-X	(I)
Construction workers	40-1 -2 -3 -4 -5 -6 -7 -8 -9 -0		-X	(I)
Jews	41-1 -2 -3 -4 -5 -6 -7 -8 -9 -0		-X	(I)
Police	42-1 -2 -3 -4 -5 -6 -7 -8 -9 -0		-X	(1)
Yourself and people like yourself	43-1 -2 -3 -4 -5 -6 -7 -8 -9 -0		-X	(I)

Q.16: How about people like yourself? On what rung of the ladder would you place yourself and people like yourself? (RECORD ABOVE)

Political Power (Bussing)

Q.20: Now, I'd like to return to one of the things we were talking about earlier — the issue of school bussing. Let's say that the top of the ladder on the yellow card I handed you represents those groups of people which city officials pay the most attention to when making decisions on bussing school children, and the bottom of the ladder represents those groups which city officials pay the least attention to. Looking again at the pink card, on which rung of the ladder would you place the different groups of people on the card? Where would you place _____ on the ladder? (ASK FOR EVERY GROUP AND RECORD ONE ANSWER FOR EACH GROUP BELOW)

Group of people	Bussing attention	Don't Know	Refuse
	(Least) ---- **(Most)**		
Union members	52-1 -2 -3 -4 -5 -6 -7 -8 -9 -0	-X	(I)
Italians	53-1 -2 -3 -4 -5 -6 -7 -8 -9 -0	-X	(I)
Medical doctors	54-1 -2 -3 -4 -5 -6 -7 -8 -9 -0	-X	(I)
Negroes	55-1 -2 -3 -4 -5 -6 -7 -8 -9 -0	-X	(I)
Irish	56-1 -2 -3 -4 -5 -6 -7 -8 -9 -0	-X	(I)
Rich people	57-1 -2 -3 -4 -5 -6 -7 -8 -9 -0	-X	(I)
Salesmen in a department store	58-1 -2 -3 -4 -5 -6 -7 -8 -9 -0	-X	(I)
People on welfare	59-1 -2 -3 -4 -5 -6 -7 -8 -9 -0	-X	(I)
Construction workers	60-1 -2 -3 -4 -5 -6 -7 -8 -9 -0	-X	(I)
Jews	61-1 -2 -3 -4 -5 -6 -7 -8 -9 -0	-X	(I)
Police	62-1 -2 -3 -4 -5 -6 -7 -8 -9 -0	-X	(I)
Yourself and people like yourself	63-1 -2 -3 -4 -5 -6 -7 -8 -9 -0	-X	(I)

Q. 21: How about people like yourself? On what rung of the ladder would you place yourself and people like yourself? (RECORD ABOVE)

Political Power (General)

Q. 59[a]: At this point I'd like to do something different. In just a minute I'm going to give you a set of cards. On each card is a statement that someone has made to us before. What I would like you to do is to read each card and then decide whether or not you agree or disagree with each statement.

(OPEN SORT BOARD AND PLACE IT IN FRONT OF THE RESPONDENT SO HE CAN READ IT)

This is how it works. As you can see, there are seven boxes. Below each box are the various words which will indicate the strength of your agreement or disagreement with each statement. When I give you the cards, I'd like you to read each one and place it in the box that comes closest to how you feel about the statement.

Now, let's try a couple of sample cards so you can see how it works.

(READ SAMPLE CARD # 1 – "I LIKE FRIED EGGS" – OUT LOUD AND THEN PLACE IT ON THE SORT BOARD ACCORDING TO HOW MUCH YOU AGREE OR DISAGREE WITH THE STATEMENT. REMEMBER TO PLACE IT SO THE RESPONDENT CAN READ IT)

Now, you take the card and place it on the board according to how much *you* agree or disagree with the statement. (LET RESPONDENT SORT CARD ON THE BOARD)

Let's try one more. (READ SAMPLE CARD # 2 – "PRESIDENT NIXON LIKES FRIED EGGS" – OUT LOUD) Well, I don't have any idea whether he likes fried eggs or not, so I would put this card here on the "not sure" box. (PLACE CARD ON "NOT SURE" BOX SO RESPONDENT CAN READ IT) Now, where would you place that card?

(LET RESPONDENT SORT CARD ON THE BOARD)

IF RESPONDENT CAN READ THE CARD AND THE BOARD, AND UNDERSTANDS THE PROCEDURE, CONTINUE AFTER COLLECTING THE TWO SAMPLE CARDS)

One other thing I should mention. We would like it if you would sort each card according to your *first reaction* to the statement.

(HAND BLUE CARD DECK. DO NOT WATCH RESPONDENT CLOSELY AFTER YOU SEE HE'S SORTING WELL. IF HE READS WELL BUT IS TAKING MORE THAN 10-15 SECONDS PER CARD,

---

[a]Sort-board adapted from questionnaire employed by the Comparative State Election Project, University of North Carolina.

REMIND HIM POLITELY THAT THE CARDS SHOULD BE SORTED
ON FIRST IMPRESSION)

(WHEN RESPONDENT FINISHES SORTING ALL 16 CARDS IN
THE BLUE DECK)

Now, if you would, I'd like you to please take all the cards you've put
on the "strongly disagree" box (POINT TO THAT BOX), turn them
over, and read the number on the back of each card to me. I'll check
off the numbers as you read them. (REPEAT FOR EACH BOX
MAKING CERTAIN THAT THE RESPONDENT PICKS UP EACH
PILE IN SEQUENCE FROM THE "STRONGLY DISAGREE" TO
THE "STRONGLY AGREE" BOX. RECORD ANSWERS ON NEXT
PAGE, MAKING SURE THAT YOU RECORD ONE AND ONLY ONE
ANSWER FOR EACH CARD. WHEN ALL CARDS ARE RECORDED
PROPERLY, COLLECT THEM)

Blue Card Deck Record

Card #	Strong-ly Dis-agree	Dis-agree	Slight-ly Dis-agree	Not Sure	Slight-ly Agree	Agree	Strong-ly Agree	Refuse	
Six(6)	66-1	-2	-3	-4	-5	-6	-7	-X	(II)
Eight (8)	68-1	-2	-3	-4	-5	-6	-7	-X	(II)
Nine (9)	69-1	-2	-3	-4	-5	-6	-7	-X	(II)
Twelve (12)	72-1	-2	-3	-4	-5	-6	-7	-X	(II)
Fifteen (15)	75-1	-2	-3	-4	-5	-6	-7	-X	(II)
Sixteen (16)	76-1	-2	-3	-4	-5	-6	-7	-X	(II)

(MAKE SURE YOU RECORD ONE AND ONLY ONE ANSWER FOR
EACH CARD. WHEN ALL CARDS ARE RECORDED PROPERLY,
COLLECT THEM AND THE SORT BOARD)

Blue Deck Cards

6.   I don't think that officials care much about what people like me think.

8.   The only people who ever get a chance to hold public office are rich.

9.   People like me don't have any say about what the government does.

12.   Voting doesn't make any difference, because after they're elected politicians always do what they want anyway.

15.   It doesn't make any difference who you vote for, because politicians don't pay any attention to people like me anyway.

16. Politicians seem to care a lot more about what big businessmen think than they do about what people like me think.

Economic (Labor)

Q. 44: What about people like yourself? Would you say that people like yourself have a better chance than other people of getting a good job, about the same chance as other people, or a worse chance than other people?

Better chance	29-1	
About the same	— 2	
Worse chance	-3	(II)
Don't know	-0	
Refuse	-X	

Subjective Affective Powerlessness

Status

Q. 17: Would you say people like yourself get more respect than you deserve, just about the right amount of respect, or less respect than you deserve? (IF ANSWER IS "MORE" OR "LESS" ASK Q. 17a. IF NOT, SKIP TO Q. 18)

More	44-1	
Right amount	-2	
Less	-3	(I)
Don't know	-0	
Refuse	-X	

Political Power (Bussing)

Q. 22: In making decisions about school bussing, would you say city officials pay more attention than deserved to people like yourself, just about the right amount of attention, or less attention than you deserve? (IF ANSWER IS "MORE" OR "LESS," ASK Q. 22a. IF NOT, SKIP TO Q. 23)

More	64-1	
Right amount	-2	
Less	-3	(I)
Don't know	-0	
Refuse	-X	

Militancy

Antigovernmental Militancy

Q. 70: Now, let's imagine that you have a child going to a school where there is nobody to help children get across a street crossing out in front. The crossing is dangerous, and one day a child is hit by a car. You think that somebody should be stationed at the crossing to help the children. So do your friends. But city officials aren't willing to do anything about it. Would you be willing to wait until city officials eventually decide to do something about the crossing or wouldn't you be willing to wait? (IF YES, ASK Q. 70a)

Yes	25-1	
No	-2	
Don't know	-0	(III)
Refuse	-X	

Q. 71: Would you write to city councilmen or other public officials to let them know how you feel about the crossing?

Yes	27-1	
No	-2	
Don't know	-0	(III)
Refuse	-X	

Q. 72: Would you contact your neighbors and friends to urge them to vote in a bloc for the city council candidate who promises to do something about the crossing? (IF YES, ASK Q. 72a)

Yes	29-1	
No	-2	
Don't know	-0	(III)
Refuse	-X	

Q. 73: Would you contribute money to the city council candidate who promises to do something about the crossing? (IF YES, ASK Q. 73a)

Yes	31-1	
No	-2	
Don't know	-0	(III)
Refuse	-X	

Q. 74: Would you attend rallies, dinners, or meetings for this candidate? (IF YES, ASK Q. 74a)

Yes	33-1	
No	-2	
Don't know	-0	(III)
Refuse	-X	

Q. 75: Would you march peaceably through town to bring the crossing to the attention of city officials? (IF YES, ASK Q. 75a)

Yes	35-1	
No	-2	
Don't know	-0	(III)
Refuse	-X	

Q. 77: Would you try to get publicity about the crossing by sitting-in at the City Hall? (IF YES, ASK Q. 77a)

Yes	39-1	
No	-2	
Don't know	-0	(III)
Refuse	-X	

Q. 78: Would you be willing to *talk* in favor of using disruptive tactics against City Hall — even if you don't really plan on doing anything violent? (IF YES, ASK Q. 78a)

Yes	41-1	
No	-2	
Don't know	-0	(III)
Refuse	-X	

Q. 79: Do you think you would *actually engage* in disruptive tactics against city property? (IF YES, ASK Q. 79a)

Yes	43-1	
No	-2	
Don't know	-0	(III)
Refuse	-X	

Q. 80: Would you go to a meeting where the Mayor was speaking and boo him? (IF YES, ASK Q. 80a)

Yes	45-1	
No	-2	
Don't know	-0	(III)
Refuse	-X	

Q. 81: Would you go to a meeting where the Mayor was speaking and carry signs about the crossing? (IF YES, ASK Q. 81a)

Yes	47-1	
No	-2	
Don't know	-0	(III)
Refuse	-X	

Q. 82: Would you go to a meeting where the Mayor was speaking and show your disapproval of his doing nothing about the crossing by throwing things at him — nothing that would hurt him? (IF YES, ASK Q. 82a)

Yes	49-1	
No	-2	
Don't know	-0	(III)
Refuse	-X	

Antiblack Militancy

Q. 36: At any time during the riot did you *consider* using a gun to protect yourself or your family?

Considered using	9-1	
Didn't consider	-2	
Don't know	-0	(II)
Refuse	-X	

Acquiescence

Antigovernmental Protestors

Q. 84: What do you think the Mayor would do if a sit-in protesting the school crossing were staged at City Hall? Do you think he would order the people arrested, try to ignore them, or would he try to do something about their demands?

Order arrested	52-1	
Ignore them	-2	
Do something about demands	-3	
Other (SPECIFY)	-4	(III)
Don't know	-0	
Refuse	-X	

Black Rioters

Q. 32: In the summer of 1967 there was a Negro riot in Roxbury. Do you think Roxbury has gotten a lot more help from the government since the riot, a little more help, or do they get about the same help now as they did before?

Lot more help	5-1	
Little more help	-2	
Same help as before	-3	(II)
Don't know	-0	
Refuse	-X	

Other

Q. 33: Do you think that the people in Roxbury were justified in rioting, should they have used other tactics to protest in a more peaceful way, or should they have waited patiently for the government to do something to help them?

Right in rioting	6-1	
More peaceful tactics	-2	
Wait for government	-3	(II)
Don't know	-0	
Refuse	-X	

Q. 34: During the 1967 Roxbury riot, did you fear for the safety of yourself or your family, or didn't you?

Felt fear	7-1	
Did not fear	-2	
Don't know	-0	(II)
Refuse	-X	

Q. 35: Did you approve of white people buying guns to protect themselves during the riot or didn't you approve of this?

Approved	8-1	
Did not approve	-2	
Don't know	-0	(II)
Refuse	-X	

Q. 36: At any time during the riot did you *consider* using a gun to protect yourself or your family?

Considered using	9-1	
Didn't consider	-2	
Don't know	-0	(II)
Refuse	-X	

Q. 37: During the riot, did you *actually buy* ammunition or a gun to protect yourself or your family?

Bought	10-1	
Did not buy	-2	
Don't know	-0	(II)
Refuse	-X	

Q. 38: Some people say that if Negroes riot in Boston, maybe whites should do some rioting against them. Others say such matters should be left entirely to the authorities to handle. Which do you think is better?

Riot against Negroes	11-1
Leave to authorities	-2
Don't know	-0
Refuse	-X

(II)

Q. 87: Where were your parents born?

55-   (III)

(COUNTRY)   (IF USA, STATE)

Q. 90: What type of work do you do? (PROBE) What is your occupation? (PROBE) Do you have a formal title at work? (PROBE) Can you describe briefly what you do at work?

58-   59-   60-   (III)

Q. 92: About how many hours do you work each week on the average?

61-   (III)

	I don't think that officials care much about what people like me think.	The only people who ever get a chance to hold public office are rich.	People like me don't have any say about what the government does.	Voting doesn't make any difference, because after they're elected politicians always do what they want anyway.	It doesn't make any difference who you vote for, because politicians don't pay any attention to people like me anyway.	Politicians seem to care a lot more about what big businessmen think than they do about what people like me think.
I don't think that officials care much about what people like me think.	—	+.40	+.48	+.50	+.47	+.41
The only people who ever get a chance to hold public office are rich.		—	+.41	+.36	+.42	+.38
People like me don't have any say about what the government does.			—	+.51	+.45	+.33
Voting doesn't make any difference, because after they're elected politicians always do what they want anyway.				—	+.63	+.37
It doesn't make any difference who you vote for, because politicians don't pay any attention to people like me anyway.					—	+.37
Politicians seem to care a lot more about what big businessmen think than they do about what people like me think.						—

Appendix E
Don't Know's and Not
Ascertained's

Attitudinal questions employed in Chapter 5 had an average "Don't Know" response of 5.7%. On only five of the thirty-one included questions did the "Don't Know" response exceed 10%:

Q. 20(55):	11.6%
Q. 21:	15.3
Q. 22:	16.9
Q. 32:	14.6
Q. 84:	10.3

Attitudinal questions employed in Chapter 5 had an average "Not Ascertained" rate of 0.8%. On no question did "Not Ascertained's" exceed 2%.

Preliminary analysis of cross-tabulation tables with D.K.'s and N.A.'s included indicated that D.K.'s and N.A.'s did not meaningfully affect our findings. In reporting our data, D.K.'s and N.A.'s were thus included only on basic frequency tables (Figure 5-1, Tables 5-3, and 5-4) and on those tables in which occupation was related to attitudes (Tables 5-15, 5-17, 5-18, 5-19, 5-22 and 5-23). D.K.'s and N.A.'s were excluded in computing Gamma's.

Notes

Preliminary Pages

1. Stephen Tracy, "The Potato Baron and the Line," *New Yorker,* 26 February 1972, p. 32.

2. Anais Nin, *The Diary of Anais Nin: 1934-1939,* Volume Two, edited by Gunther Stuhlmann (New York: Harcourt Brace Jovanovich, Inc., 1967), p. 146.

Preface

1. Karl Marx, "Theses on Feuerbach," in Lewis S. Feuer, (ed.), *Marx and Engels: Basic Writings on Politics and Philosophy* (Garden City: Anchor Books, 1959), p. 244.

2. Morris Janowitz, "Patterns of Collective Racial Violence," in Hugh Davis Graham and Ted Robert Gurr, (eds.), *Violence in America: Historical and Comparative Perspectives* (New York: Bantam Books, 1969), pp. 415-18; and Allen D. Grimshaw, "Urban Racial Violence in the United States: Changing Ecological Considerations," *American Journal of Sociology,* Volume 64 (September 1960), pp. 109-19.

3. Two important exceptions are the 1935 and 1943 Harlem riots, which resembled more closely the 1960's riots than they resembled previous American race riots. For descriptions of the Harlem riots, see: Richard Hofstadter and Michael Wallace, (eds.), *American Violence: A Documentary History* (New York: Alfred A. Knopf, 1970), pp. 258-62; Allen D. Grimshaw, (ed.), *Racial Violence in the United States* (Chicago: Aldine Publishing Company, 1969), pp. 116-28; and Anthony M. Platt, (ed.), *The Politics of Riot Commissions: 1917-1970* (New York: Collier Books, 1971), pp. 161-95.

4. Good articles concerning black attitudes toward the surrogates, and the surrogates' attitudes toward blacks, have been written by William J. Raine. See his "The Perception of Police Brutality in South Central Los Angeles," in Nathan Cohen, (ed.), *The Los Angeles Riots: A Socio-Psychological Study* (New York: Praeger Publishers, 1970), pp. 380-412; and also his "The Ghetto Merchant Study," in *ibid.,* pp. 602-37.

5. "Time to Remember 'Forgotten America,'" *Time,* 8 August 1969, pp. 42-3; "The Troubled American: A Special Report on the White Majority," *Newsweek,* 6 October 1969, pp. 29-73 (a more sophisticated analysis of the *Newsweek* data can be found in Richard Lemon, *The Troubled American* (New York: Simon and Schuster, 1970); Marshall Frady, "Gary, Indiana," *Harper's,* August, 1969, pp. 35-45.

6. Paul Goodman's 1968 article, "Reflections on Racism, Spite, Guilt, and Violence" (*New York Review of Books,* 23 May 1968, pp. 18-23) is an early exception to the white racism explanation school. See also Campbell and Schuman's eloquent criticism of the white racism explanation (Angus Campbell and Howard Schuman, "Racial Attitudes in Fifteen American Cities," in *Supplemental Studies for the National Advisory Commission on Civil Disorders* (Washington, D.C.: U.S. Government Printing Office, 1968), pp. 62-3.

7. Richard T. Morris and Vincent Jeffries, "The White Reaction Study," in Cohen, *op. cit.,* p. 503.

8. Campbell and Schuman, *op. cit.,* pp. 52 and 58.

9. *Report of the National Advisory Commission on Civil Disorders* (Washington, D.C.: U.S. Government Printing Office, 1968), p. 5. A cogent indictment of the Kerner Commission Report can be found in Gary T. Marx, "Report of the National Commission: The Analysis of Disorder or Disorderly Analysis," paper presented at the 1968 meetings of the American Political Science Association. See also Robert M. Fogelson, Gordon S. Black, and Michael Lipsky, "Review Symposium: Report of the Naitonal Advisory Commission on Civil Disorders and Supplemental Studies for the National Advisory Commission on Civil Disorders," *American Political Science Review,* Volume 63 (December 1969), pp. 1269-81.

10. The white racism and white backlash explanations gained currency despite the fact that numerous longitudinal analyses of both long- and short-term public opinion trend data demonstrate that American whites have become increasingly and consistently *more* prointegrationist since 1942. Long-term NORC data analyses include: Herbert H. Hyman and Paul B. Sheatsley, "Attitudes Toward Desegregation," *Scientific American,* Volume 195 (December 1956), pp. 35-9; Hyman and Sheatsley, "Attitudes Toward Desegregation," *Scientific American,* Volume 211 (July 1964), pp. 16-23; Sheatsley, "White Attitudes Toward the Negro," *Daedalus,* Volume 95 (Winter 1966), pp. 217-38; and Andrew M. Greeley and Sheatsley, "Attitudes Toward Racial Integration," *Scientific American,* Volume 225 (December 1971), pp. 13-9. Long-term SRC data analyses include Angus Campbell, *White Attitudes Toward Black People* (Ann Arbor: Institute for Social Research, 1971), pp. 127-54; and Richard F. Hamilton, "Black Demands, White Reactions and Liberal Alarms," in Sar A. Levitan, (ed.), *Blue-Collar Workers: A Symposium on Middle America* (New York: McGraw-Hill Book Company, 1971), pp. 130-53. Data collected in Texas throughout 1967 and 1968 indicate that — even during periods of intense racial turmoil — whites became more prointegrationist; see Thomas F. Pettigrew, "Racially Separate Or Together?," *Journal of Social Issues,* Volume 25 (January 1969), p. 53. See also Robert A. Levine, "The Silent Majority: Neither Simple Nor Simple-Minded," *Public Opinion Quarterly,* Volume 35 (Winter 1971-72), pp. 571-2.

11. Ray Marshall, "Black Workers and the Unions," *Dissent,* (Winter 1972), p. 298.

12. For discussions of the May 1970 New York demonstration see: Fred J. Cook, "Hard-Hats: The Rampaging Patriots," *Nation*, 15 June 1970, pp. 712-9; and Richard Rogin, "Joe Kelly Has Reached His Boiling Point," in Murray Friedman, (ed.), *Overcoming Middle Class Rage* (Philadelphia: The Westminster Press, 1971), pp. 66-85.

13. Alvin W. Gouldner, *The Coming Crisis of Western Sociology,* Chapter 13, "Living as a Sociologist: Toward a Reflexive Sociology," (New York: Basic Books, 1970), p. 485. Two other excellent discussions of values and objectivity in social science research are Gunnar Myrdal, *Objectivity in Social Research* (New York: Pantheon Books, 1969); and Pradeep Bandyopadhyay, "One Sociology Or Many: Some Issues in Radical Sociology," *Science and Society,* Volume 35 (Spring 1971), pp. 1-26.

14. Gouldner, *op. cit.,* p. 496.

15. Gouldner, *op. cit.*, p. 493.

16. In Ralph H. Turner's terms, I would thus classify the 1960's riots as "social protest;" see Ralph H. Turner, "The Public Perception of Protest," *American Sociological Review,* Volume 34 (December 1969), p. 816. I thus heartily endorse Robert M. Fogelson's judgment in his excellent *Violence As Protest: A Study of Riots and Ghettos* (New York: Doubleday and Company, 1971), and agree with Gary T. Marx's view that the 1960's riots generally were not "issueless." See his "Issueless Riots," in James F. Short, Jr., and Marvin E. Wolfgang, (eds.), *Collective Violence* (Chicago: Aldine-Atherton, Inc., 1972), pp. 47-59.

17. Edward C. Banfield, "Rioting Mainly for Fun and Profit," in Edward C. Banfield, *The Unheavenly City: The Nature and Future of Our Urban Crisis* (Boston: Little, Brown and Company, 1970), pp. 197-8.

18. See: Robert Nisbet, "Has Futurology a Future?," *Encounter,* November 1971, pp. 18-28; Myrdal, *op. cit.,* pp. 47-9; Norman Birnbaum, "The Crisis in Marxist Sociology," in Hans Peter Dreitzell, (ed.), *Recent Sociology,* Number 1 (London: The Macmillan Company, 1969), pp. 12-42; and Jerzy J. Wiatr, "Sociology-Marxism-Reality," in Peter L. Berger, (ed.), *Marxism and Sociology: Views from Eastern Europe* (New York: Appleton-Century-Crofts, 1969), pp. 18-36.

19. Georg Lukacs, "What Is Orthodox Marxism?," in Georg Lukacs, *History and Class Consciousness: Studies in Marxist Dialectics,* translated by Rodney Livingstone (Cambridge: The MIT Press, 1971), p. 6.

20. W.G. Runciman, *Relative Deprivation and Social Justice: A Study of Attitudes to Social Inequality in Twentieth Century England* (Berkeley: University of California Press, 1966), p. 6.

21. Two of these exceptions are the recent works by Runciman (*op. cit.*) and John C. Leggett, *Class, Race, and Labor: Working Class Consciousness in Detroit* (New York: Oxford University Press, 1968). I am particularly indebted to Runciman's work.

Chapter 1

Marx's Questions about Militancy

1. Reprinted with the permission of Farrar, Straus and Giroux, Inc. from *Everything That Rises Must Converge* by Flannery O'Connor, copyright © 1964, 1965 by the Estate of Mary Flannery O'Connor.

2. See Marx's "Enquête Ouvrière," in *Karl Marx: Selected Writings in Sociology and Social Philosophy,* edited by T.B. Bottomore and Maximilien Rubel (New York: McGraw-Hill, 1956), pp. 203-12.

3. C. Wright Mills, *The Marxists* (New York: Dell Publishing Company, 1962), pp. 84-95; Ralf Dahrendorf, *Class and Class Conflict in Industrial Society* (Stanford: Stanford University Press, 1959), pp. 32-5. See also Lawrence E. Hazelrigg, "Class, Property, and Authority: Dahrendorf's Critique of Marx's Theory of Class," *Social Forces,* Volume 50 (June 1972), pp. 473-87.

4. Karl Marx and Friedrich Engels, *The German Ideology* (New York: International Publishers, 1947), pp. 16-7.

5. Karl Marx, *Wage-Labour and Capital* (New York: International Publishers, 1933), p. 33. See also *ibid.,* p. 39.

6. Karl Marx, *Capital: A Critique of Political Economy,* Volume One, edited by Friedrich Engels and translated by Samuel Morse and Edward Aveling, (New York: International Publishers, 1967), p. 652. Marx makes similar statements in *ibid.,* p. 613 and p. 620, and in *Wage-Labour and Capital, op. cit.,* p. 40. As with almost everything else, Marx is somewhat inconsistent on this point, and occasionally prophesizes a decline in wages that is both absolute and relative. Thus, see *Capital, op. cit.,* p. 645 and p. 763.

7. *Ibid.,* p. 613.

8. *Ibid.,* p. 620. See also *ibid.,* p. 618: "a rise in the price of labour, as a consequence of accumulation of capital, only means, in fact, that the length and weight of the golden chain the wage-worker has already forged for himself, allow of a relaxation of the tension of it."

9. Marx also asserts that job insecurity, as well as alienation, is a major fault inherent in the capitalist economy. He seems to believe that such insecurity varies independently of wage increases: wages could rise at the same time that jobs become less secure.

10. Karl Marx and Friedrich Engels, *The Communist Manifesto* (New York: Monthly Review Press, 1964), p. 3.

11. *Ibid.,* p. 15.

12. *Ibid.,* p. 20.

13. Marx, *Capital, op. cit.,* p. 626.

14. Marx clearly defines productive labor in *The Grundrisse* (Karl Marx, *The Grundrisse,* edited and translated by David McLellan, New York: Harper and

Row, 1971, p. 79n): "Productive labour is simply labour that produces capital. Is it not absurd, asks Mr. Senior, . . . that the piano-maker is regarded as a productive worker, but not the pianist, although without the pianist the piano would have no meaning? But this is exactly the position. The piano-maker reproduces capital; the pianist merely exchanges his labour for income. But the pianist produces music and satisfies our musical sense; perhaps to some extent he produces this sense. In fact he does this: his work does produce something, but it is not therefore productive labour in the economic sense, any more than the work of a madman is productive when he produces hallucinations."

15. Marx, *Capital, op. cit.,* p. 445.

16. *Ibid.,* p. 420.

17. *Ibid.,* p. 446. Marx also comments on the growing number of "ideological" workers in his *The Eighteenth Brumaire of Louis Bonaparte* (New York: International Publishers, 1963), p. 129.

18. See Karl Marx, *The Civil War in France* (New York: International Publishers, 1968), p. 62; and Karl Marx, *Class Struggles in France: 1848-1850* (New York: International Publishers, 1964), pp. 123-4.

19. See Marx, *Capital, op. cit.,* pp. 642-3.

20. *Ibid.,* and Marx and Engels, *Manifesto, op. cit.,* pp. 15-6.

21. Marx, *Eighteenth Brumaire, op. cit.,* p. 75; Marx, *Capital, op. cit.,* p. 446.

22. Karl Marx, *The Poverty of Philosophy* (New York: International Publishers, 1963), p. 173. See also Marx and Engels, *German Ideology, op. cit.,* pp. 48-9.

23. Marx, *Eighteenth Brumaire, op. cit.,* p. 124.

24. *Ibid.*

25. Karl Marx, "Introduction," *Contribution to the Critique of Hegel's Philosophy of Right,* in T.B. Bottomore, editor and translator, *Karl Marx: Early Writings* (New York: McGraw-Hill, 1963), p. 56.

26. Marx, *Wage-Labour, op. cit.,* p. 33.

27. Herbert Marcuse, *Soviet Marxism: A Critical Analysis* (New York: Vintage Books, 1961), p. 12.

28. Marx, "Introduction," *op. cit.,* p. 58.

29. Karl Marx, *Critique of the Gotha Programme* (New York: International Publishers, 1966), p. 12.

30. Marx and Engels, *German Ideology, op. cit.,* p. 69.

31. Stanislaw Ossowski, *Class Structure in the Social Consciousness,* translated by Sheila Patterson (New York: The Free Press, 1963), p. 83: "the dichotomic aspect of the Marxian theory of classes indicates the direction in which capitalist societies will develop; seen in this perspective the multi-divisional schemes are intended to refer to transitory phenomena."

32. Marx, *Class Struggles, op. cit.,* p. 124.

33. Marx, *Eighteenth Brumaire, op. cit.,* p. 128.

34. See David O. Sears, "The Political Attitudes of Los Angeles Negroes," in Cohen, *op. cit.,* pp. 690-2; and David O. Sears, "Black Attitudes Toward the Political System in the Aftermath of the Watts Insurrection," *Midwest Journal of Political Science,* Volume 13 (November 1969), pp. 515-44.

35. Marx to Friedrich Bolte, 23 November 1871, in Karl Marx and Friedrich Engels, *The Selected Correspondence of Karl Marx and Frederick Engels: 1846-1895* (New York: International Publishers, 1942), p. 318.

36. *Ibid.,* pp. 318-9. Marx made a strikingly similar comment more than twenty years earlier in *The Poverty of Philosophy, op. cit.,* pp. 172-3.

37. Avineri's discussion of this point is particularly good. See Shlomo Avineri, *The Social and Political Thought of Karl Marx* (Cambridge: Cambridge University Press, 1968), pp. 188-91.

38. Marx, *Poverty of Philosophy, op. cit.,* p. 175 and p. 230. Marx made a similar comment during the previous year in *The German Ideology, op. cit.,* p. 191.

39. Marx, *Civil War in France, op. cit.,* p. 34.

40. Karl Marx, Address to the Hague Congress of the First International, 18 September 1872, quoted in Avineri, *op. cit.,* p. 216.

41. In his *Marxism: An Historical and Critical Survey* (New York: Frederick A. Praeger, Inc., 1964, p. 129), Lichtheim comments: ". . . Marx in the end evolved a political outlook which fitted the requirements of the modern age. In this mature conception, labour's conquest of power represents an aspect of the struggle for democracy. . . . Democratic socialism takes its place alongside democratic liberalism as the universally recognised expression of labour's slow rise to maturity and power." See also Seymour Martin Lipset, "Is Gradual Change Possible?," in Michael Curtis, (ed.), *Marxism* (New York: Atherton Press, 1970), pp. 275-9.

42. As late as 19 September 1879, Marx indirectly indicates his support for violence in a letter to Friedrich Sorge (Karl Marx and Friedrich Engels, *Letters to Americans, 1848-1895: A Selection* (New York: International Publishers, 1953), p. 120. See also Marx's famous 12 April 1871 letter to Dr. Kugelmann *(Selected Correspondence, op. cit.,* p. 309).

43. Marx adopted a similar stance in judging the morality of all violence. In his 1856 work the *Secret Diplomatic History of the Eighteenth Century* (New York: International Publishers, 1969, p. 85), Marx comments: "to judge Governments and their acts, we must measure them by their own times and the conscience of their contemporaries."

Chapter 2

Marx and Survey Research on Militancy

1. From V.O. Key and Frank Munger, "Social Determinism and Electoral

Decision: The Case of Indiana," in *American Voting Behavior,* edited by Eugene Burdick and Arthur J. Brodbeck (© 1959 by The Free Press (of Glencoe, Illinois), A Corporation), p. 299.

2. See Nathan Caplan, "The New Ghetto Man: A Review of Recent Empirical Studies," *Journal of Social Issues,* Volume 26 (Winter 1970), pp. 59-73, for a fine review of attitudinal studies on the black riots. Other relevant review articles include: Allen D. Grimshaw, "Interpreting Collective Violence: An Argument for the Importance of Social Structure," in Short and Wolfgang, *op. cit.,* pp. 35-46; Peter Lupsha, "On Theories of Urban Violence," paper presented before the 1968 meetings of the American Political Science Association; Gary T. Marx, "Issueless Riots," *op. cit.;* and Clark McPhail, "Civil Disorder Participation: A Critical Examination of Recent Research," *American Sociological Review,* Volume 36 (December 1971), pp. 1058-73.

3. Allen D. Grimshaw, "Three Views of Urban Violence: Civil Disturbance, Racial Revolt, Class Assault," in Louise H. Masotti and Don R. Bowen, (eds.), *Riots and Rebellion: Civil Violence in the Urban Community* (Beverly Hills: Sage Publications, 1968), pp. 103-19. For an excellent review of the assumptions lying behind American race relations literature, see L. Paul Metzger, "American Sociology and Black Assimiliation: Conflicting Perspectives," *American Journal of Sociology,* Volume 76 (January 1971), pp. 627-47.

4. James A. Geschwender, "Civil Rights Protest and Riots: A Disappearing Distinction," *Social Science Quarterly,* Volume 49 (December 1968), p. 474.

5. Kenneth B. Clark, "Group Violence: A Preliminary Study of the Attitudinal Pattern of Its Acceptance and Rejection: A Study of the 1943 Harlem Riot," in Allen D. Grimshaw, (ed.), *Racial Violence in the United States* (Chicago: Aldine Publishing Company, 1969), pp. 421-33.

6. David C. Schwartz, "Urban Political Alienation: Ethnic Differences and Violent Consequences," paper presented at the 1969 meetings of the American Political Science Association, p. 17; David O. Sears and John B. McConahay, "The Politics of Discontent," in Cohen, *op. cit.,* p. 431.

7. Sears and McConahay, "The Politics of Discontent," *op. cit.,* pp. 429-30; Jeffrey M. Paige, "Political Orientation and Riot Participation," *American Sociological Review,* Volume 36 (October 1971), pp. 817-8; and Joel D. Aberbach and Jack L. Walker, "Political Trust and Racial Ideology," *American Political Science Review,* Volume 64 (December 1970), p. 1213. Paige, and Sears and McConahay use questions which directly tap riot participation; Aberbach and Walker use a projective question.

8. Benjamin D. Singer, Richard W. Osborn, and James A. Geschwender, *Black Rioters: A Study of Social Factors and Communication in the Detroit Riot* (Lexington, Mass.: D.C. Heath and Company, 1970), p. 85; Nathan S. Caplan and Jeffrey M. Paige, "A Study of Ghetto Rioters," *Scientific American,* Volume 219 (August 1968), p. 20. See also Don R. Bowen, Elinor Bowen, Sheldon Gawiser, and Louis H. Masotti, "Deprivation, Mobility, and Orientation Toward Protest of the Urban Poor," in Masotti and Bowen, *op. cit.,* pp. 187-200; this interesting article is based upon a Cleveland sample containing

both whites and blacks, and separate analyses are not performed for the different racial groups.

9. Paul D. Wellstone, "Black Militants in the Ghetto: Why They Believe in Violence" (doctoral dissertation, Chapel Hill: Department of Political Science, University of North Carolina, 1969), p. 62; H. Edward Ransford, "Isolation, Powerlessness, and Violence: A Study of Attitudes and Participation in the Watts Riot," *American Journal of Sociology,* Volume 73 (March 1968), pp. 581-91; Caplan and Paige, *op. cit.,* p. 20. Interestingly, Caplan and Paige report no relationship between riot participation and perception of a widening economic gap between blacks and whites; Singer et al., *op. cit.,* pp. 86-8, display related and similar data.

10. Caplan and Paige, *op. cit.,* pp. 17 and 20; David O. Sears and John B. McConahay, "Racial Socialization, Comparison Levels, and the Watts Riot," *Journal of Social Issues,* Volume 26 (Winter 1970), pp. 136-7. Caplan and Paige report the occupational aspirations finding. Wellstone, *op. cit.,* p. 61, reports a contrary relationship. For findings on related dissatisfactions, see Campbell and Schuman, *op. cit.,* pp. 57-8.

11. Raymond J. Murphy and James M. Watson, "The Structure of Discontent: The Relationship Between Social Structure, Grievance, and Riot Support," in Cohen, *op. cit.,* p. 185.

12. Harlan Hahn, "The Political Objectives of Ghetto Violence," paper presented at the 1969 meetings of the American Political Science Association, p. 13; Murphy and Watson, *op. cit.,* p. 186. See also: Singer et al., *op. cit.,* pp. 30-5; Campbell and Schuman, *op. cit.,* p. 58; and David H. Bayley and Harold Mendelsohn, *Minorities and the Police: Confrontation in America* (New York: The Free Press, 1969), pp. 179-81.

13. Charles H. Moore, "The Politics of Urban Violence: Policy Outcomes in Winston-Salem, North Carolina," paper presented at the 1969 meetings of the American Political Science Association, pp. 19-20; Sears and McConahay, "Racial Socialization, Comparison Levels, and the Watts Riot," *op. cit.,* pp. 131-3; and Hahn, "Political Objectives of Ghetto Violence," *op. cit.,* p. 11. See also Sears, "Political Attitudes of Los Angeles Negroes," *op. cit.,* pp. 676-705, and Sears, "Black Attitudes Toward the Political System in the Aftermath of the Watts Insurrection," *op. cit.,* pp. 515-44. Sears and McConahay's "Racial Socialization, Comparison Levels, and the Watts Riot," *op. cit.,* pp. 132-3, contains fascinating contrasting findings: rioters, while more likely to dislike local governmental policies, are no more likely than non-rioters to dislike the national government.

14. *Report of the National Advisory Commission on Civil Disorders, op. cit.,* p. 75; Clark, *op. cit.,* pp. 424-5; Wellstone, *op. cit.,* pp. 50-1; Jay Schulman, "Ghetto-Area Residence, Political Alienation, and Riot Orientation," in Masotti and Bowen, *op. cit.,* pp. 261-84; Gary T. Marx, *Protest and Prejudice: A Study of Belief in the Black Community* (New York: Harper Torchbooks, 1969), p. 56.

15. Singer et al., *op. cit.*, p. 58.

16. Campbell and Schuman, *op. cit.*, pp. 56-7 (for a good general critique of Campbell and Schuman's study, see Harlan Hahn, "Ghetto Sentiments on Violence," *Science and Society*, Volume 32 (Spring 1968), pp. 197-208), Murphy and Watson, *op. cit.*, p. 222. The strength of the reported relationships between militancy and education varies greatly; see McPhail, *op. cit.*, p. 1069n, for further comments on this inconsistency.

17. Gary Marx, *op. cit.*, p. 57; Caplan and Paige, *op. cit.*, p. 17; Murphy and Watson, *op. cit.*, p. 223. Once again, the strength of these relationships varies greatly. The relationship reported by Gary Marx is particularly strong; this may be due to the nature of his "Index of Conventional Militancy," which includes questions on protesting and demonstrating, but not rioting. For other data on occupation and riot participation, see Singer et al., *op. cit.*, pp. 61-4; in a fascinating finding, they report that ". . . the arrestee sample, compared to those in the community, have achieved a lower occupational rank for a given level of education [*ibid.*, p. 64]." See also Geschwender, "Civil Rights Protest and Riots," *op. cit.*, p. 482.

18. Murphy and Watson, *op. cit.*, p. 224; Caplan and Paige, *op. cit.*, p. 17; again, the strength of these relationships varies, and Caplan and Paige find no such relationship in Detroit. See also Singer et al., *op. cit.*, p. 64.

19. James F. Kirkham, Sheldon G. Levy, and William J. Crotty, *Assassination and Political Violence: A Staff Report to the National Commission on the Causes and Prevention of Violence* (Washington, D.C.: U.S. Government Printing Office, 1969), p. 215.

20. Campbell, *op. cit.*, pp. 109-10.

21. Marvin E. Olsen, "Perceived Legitimacy of Social Protest Actions," *Social Problems*, Volume 15 (Winter 1968), pp. 300-3; Schwartz, *op. cit.*, p. 19.

22. Campbell, *op. cit.*, pp. 35-6.

23. Vincent Jeffries, Ralph H. Turner, and Richard T. Morris, "The Public Perception of the Watts Riot as Social Protest," *American Sociological Review*, Volume 36 (June 1971), p. 449. See also the excellent study by Monica D. Blumenthal, Robert L. Kahn, Frank M. Andrews, and Kendra B. Head, *Justifying Violence: Attitudes of American Men* (Ann Arbor: Institute for Social Research, 1972), pp. 61-2, and pp. 164-5. Unfortunately, for us, Blumenthal et al. report few findings separately for the whites in their sample.

24. Campbell, *op. cit.*, pp. 108-12. A good explanation of the common cause reasoning can be found in Jeffries, Turner, and Morris, *op. cit.*, pp. 446-8.

25. Morris and Jeffries, *op. cit.*, pp. 505-6; Campbell and Schuman, *op. cit.*, p. 59; Campbell, *op. cit.*, pp. 57 and 60.

26. Campbell, *op. cit.*, p. 52; Morris and Jeffries, *op. cit.*, p. 507. Once again, these data are neither clear nor linear. However, averaging averages across occupational categories yields the following: Morris and Jeffries — 35.5% middle class consider using firearms, 43% blue-collar; Campbell — 3% middle class

condone counter-rioting, 7% blue-collar.

27. Sheldon G. Levy, "Response Orientation to Governmental Injustice," paper delivered at the 1969 meeting of the Midwest Psychology Association, pp. 23-40; Olsen, *op. cit.,* pp. 300-1. See also Levy, "Special Research Report," in Kirkham, Levy, and Crotty, *op. cit.,* pp. 402-16.

28. Paige, *op. cit.,* artfully employs Gamson's model. Singer et al., *op. cit.,* pp. 89-96, and Campbell and Schuman, *op. cit.,* pp. 51-6, also present some data on this point. See also: Levy, "Special Research Report," *op. cit.,* and Sheldon G. Levy, "The Psychology of the Politically Violent," paper delivered at the 1969 meetings of the Pacific Sociology Association.

29. David O. Sears and John B. McConahay, "Participation in the Los Angeles Riot," *Social Problems,* Volume 17 (Summer 1969), pp. 9-10.

30. Singer et al., *op. cit.,* p. 17, make a similar criticism.

31. For example, Wellstone's "Militancy Scale" and Gary Marx's "Index of Conventional Militancy."

Chapter 3

Building a Theory of Militancy

1. Georg Lukacs, "What Is Orthodox Marxism?" *op. cit.,* p. 1.

2. Richard Centers, *The Psychology of Social Classes* (Princeton: Princeton University Press, 1949). Centers' book has been discussed and criticized by many sociologists, including: Llewellyn Gross ("The Use of Class Concepts in Sociological Research," *American Journal of Sociology,* Volume 54 (January 1949), pp. 418-9); Herman M. Case ("Marxian Implications of Centers' Interest-Group Theory: A Critical Appraisal," *Social Forces,* Volume 33 (March 1955), pp. 255-6); Milton M. Gordon (*Social Class in American Sociology,* New York: McGraw-Hill Book Company, Inc., 1958, pp. 193-202); H.J. Eysenck ("Social Attitude and Social Class," *British Journal of Sociology,* Volume 1 (March 1950), pp. 58-9); and Joseph A. Kahl (*The American Class Structure,* New York: Rinehart and Company, Inc., 1957, pp. 163-4).

3. Attitudinal studies of class consciousness within the United States include: Herman M. Case, "An Independent Test of the Interest-Group Theory of Social Class," *American Sociological Review,* Volume 17 (December 1952), pp. 751-5; Neal Gross, "Social Class Identification in the Urban Community," *American Sociological Review,* Volume 18 (August 1953), pp. 398-404; John L. Haer, "An Empirical Study of Social Class Awareness," *Social Forces,* Volume 36 (December 1957), pp. 117-21; Joseph A. Kahl and James A. Davis, "A Comparison of Indexes of Socio-Economic Status," *American Sociological*

Review, Volume 20 (June 1955), pp. 317-25; Jerome G. Manis and Bernard N. Meltzer, "Attitudes of Textile Workers to Class Structure," *American Journal of Sociology*, Volume 60 (July 1954), pp. 30-5; Jerome G. Manis and Bernard N. Meltzer, "Some Correlates of Class Consciousness Among Textile Workers," *American Journal of Sociology*, Volume 69 (September 1963), pp. 177-84; Oscar Glantz, "Class Consciousness and Political Solidarity," *American Sociological Review*, Volume 23 (August 1958), pp. 375-83; and Leggett, *op. cit.*

4. Marx, *Wage-Labour and Capital, op. cit.*, p. 33.

5. Max Weber, "Class, Status, Party," H.H. Gerth and C. Wright Mills, (eds.), *From Max Weber: Essays in Sociology* (New York: Oxford University Press, 1946), p. 180.

6. *Ibid.*

7. *Ibid.*, p. 187.

8. *Ibid.*, pp. 186-7.

9. *Ibid.*, p. 194.

10. *Ibid.*, p. 181.

11. *Ibid.*, p. 193.

12. *Ibid.*, p. 182. Substantial disagreement exists among scholars concerning the similarity between the Marxian and Weberian definitions of class. See: Oliver C. Cox, "Max Weber on Social Stratification: A Critique," *American Sociological Review*, Volume 15 (April 1950), pp. 223-4; and Reinhard Bendix, *Max Weber: An Intellectual Portrait* (New York: Anchor Books, 1962), p. 86.

13. Weber, *op. cit.*, p. 185. Weber refers to the first hierarchy as "consumption credit," the second as "price wars on the labor market," and the third as the "commodity market." For an excellent discussion of these three hierarchies, and an attempt to apply them to American history, see Norbert Wiley, "America's Unique Class Politics: The Interplay of the Labor, Credit and Commodity Markets," *American Sociological Review*, Volume 32 (August 1967), pp. 529-41.

14. Weber, *op. cit.*, p. 194.

15. *Ibid.*

16. This discussion could be extended to my suggested redefinition of Weber's "party" dimension.

17. Weber, *op. cit.*, p. 184.

18. Irving M. Zeitlin, "The Plain Marxism of C. Wright Mills," in George Fischer, (ed.), *The Revival of American Socialism: Selected Papers of the Socialist Scholars Conference* (New York: Oxford University Press, 1971), p. 230.

19. See Marx to Siegfried Meyer and August Vogt, 9 April 1870, in Marx and Engels, *Letters to Americans, op. cit.*, pp. 77-80; and Karl Marx, *Revolution and Counter-Revolution*, edited by Eleanor Marx Aveling (New York: Capricorn Books, 1956), pp. 44-7.

20. Paulo Freire, *Pedagogy of the Oppressed,* translated by Myra Bergman Ramos (New York: Herder and Herder, 1970), p. 34. The Rolling Stones say "the time is right for violent revolution," but they then ask "what can a poor boy do but play for a rock and roll band?"

21. Arthur Kornhauser, "Public Opinion and Social Class," *American Journal of Sociology,* Volume 55 (January 1950), p. 339. Reprinted with the permission of the University of Chicago Press.

22. Marx, *The Grundrisse, op. cit.,* p. 79.

23. In the following discussion I am heavily indebted to: Werner S. Landecker, "Class Crystallization and Class Consciousness," *American Sociological Review,* Volume 28 (April 1963), pp. 219-29; and to Giovanni Sartori, "From the Sociology of Politics to Political Sociology," in Seymour M. Lipset, (ed.), *Politics and the Social Sciences* (New York: Oxford University Press, 1969), pp. 65-100.

24. Thus, Lenski employs the occupational prestige scale developed by NORC to place his respondents in an occupational status hierarchy. See Gerhard E. Lenski, "Status Crystallization: A Non-Vertical Dimension of Social Status," *American Sociological Review,* Volume 19 (August 1954), pp. 406-7.

25. Runciman, *op. cit.,* p. 10.

26. *Ibid.*

27. Georges Sorel, *Reflections on Violence,* translated by T.E. Hulme and J. Roth (Copyright 1950 by The Free Press, A Corporation), pp. 81-92, *passim.* Neil J. Smelser, in his *Theory of Collective Behavior* (New York: The Free Press, 1962), pp. 231-5 and pp. 261-8, similarly discusses how agencies of social control which weakly or inconsistently respond to hostile outbursts could stimulate even more violence.

28. Ted Robert Gurr, *Why Men Rebel* (Princeton: Princeton University Press, 1970), p. 211.

29. William A. Gamson, *Power and Discontent* (Homewood, Ill.: The Dorsey Press, 1968), p. 173.

30. Weber, *op. cit.,* p. 184.

31. Sorel, *op. cit.,* p. 48.

32. Gurr, *op. cit.,* p. 201.

Chapter 4

Background of the Militancy Research

1. James Agee and Walker Evans, *Let Us Now Praise Famous Men* (Boston: Houghton Mifflin Company, 1960), pp. 7-8.

2. Office of Economic Opportunity-National Science Foundation dissertation research on poverty grant, NSF Grant No. GS-3011; National Science

Foundation Center for Excellence Research Award.

3. Good general descriptions of Massachusetts political history are contained in J. Joseph Huthmacher, *Massachusetts People and Politics: 1919-1933* (New York: Atheneum Books, 1959), and, for a history of more recent events, Edgar Litt, *The Political Cultures of Massachusetts* (Cambridge: The MIT Press, 1965). For an excellent social history of the nineteenth century Boston immigrant population, see Oscar Handlin, *Boston's Immigrants: A Study in Acculturation,* revised edition (New York: Atheneum Books, 1959). A highly sympathetic and revealing portrait of twentieth century Boston immigrant politics is Edwin O'Connor's *The Last Hurrah* (New York: Bantam Books, 1956); an equally good social portrait of the Boston Irish is his *The Edge of Sadness* (New York: Bantam Books, 1961).

4. A clear explanation of the confusing history of the Racial Imbalance Act can be found in Peter Schrag, *Village School Downtown: Boston Schools, Boston Politics* (Boston: Beacon Press, 1967); and Frank Levy, *Northern Schools and Civil Rights: The Racial Imbalance Act of Massachusetts* (Chicago: Markham Publishing Company, 1971). Unless otherwise specified, the account of the Racial Imbalance Act is based upon Levy and Schrag, as well as the 1965-72 *Boston Globe* and *New York Times.*

5. *Boston Globe,* 9 November 1971, p. 6.

6. *Boston Globe,* 2 December 1971, p. 26.

7. *Boston Globe,* 9 November 1971, p. 6.

8. This account is based on *Boston Globe* and *New York Times* articles appearing during June 1967, April 1968, and September 1968.

9. *New York Times,* 6 June 1967, p. 36.

10. *New York Times,* 11 June 1967, p. 80.

11. *New York Times,* 29 September 1968, p. 45.

12. Schrag, *op. cit.,* p. 17.

13. Thomas F. Pettigrew, *Racially Separate Or Together?* (New York: McGraw-Hill Book Company, 1971), p. 214.

14. Berkeley Rice, "Boston — 'I Am A Symbol of Resistance' — Hicks," *New York Times Magazine,* 5 November 1967, p. 125.

15. *Ibid.*

16. *New York Times,* 27 September 1967, p. 34. Marx would have shuddered.

17. Rice, *op. cit.,* p. 122.

18. *Ibid.,* p. 128.

19. Tom Wicker, "In the Nation: Boston Faces A Choice," *New York Times,* Section 4, 27 August 1967, p. 14.

20. *New York Times,* 24 September 1967, p. 83.

21. Hicks' handling of the police issue may have contributed to her defeat in the 1967 mayoralty election. Hicks suggested that police authority could be

increased through raising the minimum wage of patrolmen to $10,000. Increased wages for city employees meant increases in Boston's already high property taxes. The price of increased power was apparently too high.

22. *New York Times,* 24 September 1967, p. 83; Rice, *op. cit.,* p. 31; Tom Wicker, "In the Nation: Frontlash and Backlash," *New York Times,* 5 October 1967, p. 38; "Backlash in Boston – And Across the U.S.," *Newsweek,* 6 November 1967, p. 29. Wicker viewed Hicks as handling the backlash with discretion, and maintained that backlash alone would not be enough to unite her many supporters.

23. Pettigrew, *Racially Separate Or Together?, op. cit.,* pp. 216, 218, 224. Pettigrew also details fascinating data demonstrating that Hicks' strongest supporters are more likely than her opponents to send their children to Boston public schools and to own their own homes (*ibid.,* pp. 222-3).

24. *New York Times,* 24 September 1967, p. 83. Much of the criticism directed at Hicks has been founded on the premise that she succeeds through manipulating and drawing upon the conservative and racist feelings of her lower-middle class and working class white ethnic constituency. On a local scale, Pettigrew's data – at least regarding the antineighborhood and school integrationist sentiment of many of her supporters – seem to bear this out partially. Yet other data, collected both in Boston and nationwide, serve to remind us that such generalizations should be made only cautiously. Thus, James Q. Wilson and Edward C. Banfield, in a survey of Boston home-owners, find that ". . . Irish and Polish Catholic respondents with relatively low incomes and little schooling were more likely to be good government-minded than benefit-minded [James Q. Wilson and Edward C. Banfield, "Political Ethos Revisited," *American Political Science Review,* Volume 65 (December 1971), p. 1062] ." Also, Father Andrew M. Greeley of the National Opinion Research Center has discovered that Irish Catholics are second only to Jews in their support for black demands for integration. See Andrew M. Greeley, *That Most Distressful Nation: The Taming of the American Irish* (Chicago: Quadrangle Books, 1972), pp. 219-20; and Andrew M. Greeley, "Political Attitudes Among American White Ethnics," *Public Opinion Quarterly,* Volume 36 (Summer 1972), pp. 213-20.

25. *New York Times,* 7 May 1967, p. 52.

26. *Boston Sunday Globe,* 24 October 1971, p. 24.

27. Runciman, *op. cit.,* pp. 151-244.

28. Stanley A. Hetzler, "An Investigation of the Distinctiveness of Social Classes," *American Sociological Review,* Volume 18 (October 1953), pp. 493-7.

29. Hadley Cantril, *The Pattern of Human Concerns* (New Brunswick, N.J.: Rutgers University Press, 1965), pp. 21-9. After a draft of the interview schedule was completed, Ted Gurr indicated to me that he and his colleagues at Princeton had employed a somewhat similar adaptation of the Cantril self-anchoring scale. See Harry Eckstein, Ted Gurr, Joel Prager, and Ron Rogowski, "Inequality Dimensions: Distance, Bases of Distance, Deportment" (unpublished manuscript, Princeton: Workship in Comparative Politics, OP-06, June 1967); and

Harry Eckstein and Ted Gurr, "Consolidated Interview and Questionnaire Schedules" (unpublished manuscript, Princeton: Workshop in Comparative Politics, December 1967).

30. In their excellent and stimulating research, William H. Form and Joan H. Rytina ("Ideological Beliefs on the Distribution of Power in the United States," *American Sociological Review,* Volume 34 (February 1969), pp. 19-31; and Joan H. Rytina, William H. Form, and John Pease, "Income and Stratification Ideology: Beliefs About the American Opportunity Structure," *American Journal of Sociology,* Volume 75 (January 1970), pp. 703-16) use a somewhat similar technique. See also Reeve D. Vanneman and Thomas F. Pettigrew, "Race and Relative Deprivation in the Urban United States," *Race,* Volume 13 (April 1972), pp. 461-86.

31. See Joel D. Aberbach, "Alienation and Political Behavior," *American Political Science Review,* Volume 63 (March 1969), p. 92; John E. Horton and Wayne E. Thompson, "Political Alienation as a Force in Political Action," *Social Forces,* Volume 38 (March 1960), pp. 191-2;

32. Unfortunately, no questions were asked pertaining to the subjective affective level of the economic class dimension.

33. Donald R. Matthews and James W. Prothro, *Negroes and the New Southern Politics* (New York: Harcourt, Brace and World, Inc., 1966), p. 526, and pp. 503-4.

34. In the pretest questionnaires, more extreme militant actions were included in this series of questions. However, willingness to use these means was all but nonexistent among the respondents, and the items were eliminated from the final interview schedule.

Chapter 5

Research Findings on Militancy

1. From "The Crisis in Marxist Sociology" by Norman Birnbaum, Volume 25, Number 2, (Summer 1968) *Social Research,* pp. 348-80. This article also appears in Norman Birnbaum, *Toward a Critical Sociology* (New York: Oxford University Press, 1971).

2. For example, see: Daniel Bell, "The Dispossessed," in Daniel Bell, (ed.), *The Radical Right* (New York: Anchor Books, 1963), pp. 1-45; Seymour Martin Lipset, "The Sources of the 'Radical Right,' " in *ibid,* pp. 307-71; and Seymour Martin Lipset, "Fascism — Left, Right, and Center," in Seymour Martin Lipset, *Political Man: The Social Bases of Politics* (New York: Anchor Books, 1960), pp. 127-79.

3. Marx to Vera Zasulich, 8 March 1881, in Karl Marx, *Pre-Capitalist Economic Formations,* translated by Jack Cohen (New York: International Publishers, 1964), p. 145.

4. Engels to Joseph Bloch, 21 September 1890, in *Selected Correspondence, op. cit.,* p. 475.

5. The reasoning in this section draws heavily upon David M. Potter, *People of Plenty: Economic Abundance and the American Character* (Chicago: University of Chicago Press, 1954), pp. 91-110; and Seymour Martin Lipset, *The First New Nation: The United States in Historical and Comparative Perspective* (New York: Anchor Books, 1963), pp. 366-402.

6. "Backlash in Boston – And Across the U.S.," *Newsweek,* 6 November 1967, p. 29.

7. Jerome H. Skolnick, *The Politics of Protest* (New York: Ballantine Books, 1969), pp. 210-40.

8. *Boston Globe,* 3 November 1971, p. 27.

9. *Report of the National Advisory Commission on Civil Disorders, op. cit.,* p. 20 and p. 325.

10. See Ted R. Gurr, *op. cit.,* pp. 210-23.

11. This speculation on the intensity with which views are held and militancy cannot be tested with the Boston data. Devising measures of intensity would involve a two-stage Likert-type technique. First, respondents would have to state the extent to which they agree or disagree with a stated end. Second, they would have to say how intense their agreement or disagreement is, *relative* to other agreements or disagreements concerning ends. An individual could strongly disagree with the statement that "Negroes were right in rioting," yet whether or not the Roxbury riots were justified may be relatively unimportant to him compared to his strong disagreement with federal income tax policy.

12. Morris and Jeffries, *op. cit.,* pp. 506-7; Campbell and Schuman, *op. cit.,* p. 59; Campbell, *op. cit.,* p. 52 and p. 60.

13. Supporting data regarding the effect of education on antigovernmental militancy can be found in Levy, "Special Research Report," *op. cit.,* pp. 407-10; and Olsen, *op. cit.,* p. 301.

14. The argument, of course, is a take-off from Lipset. See his *Political Man, op. cit.,* pp. 106-7 and pp. 114-6.

15. Lemon (*op. cit.,* p. 167) finds that 46% of blue-collar workers, compared to 38% of the "rich," agree that "Negroes today have a better chance . . . than people like yourself to get a good education for their children." Similarly, Pettigrew points out (Pettigrew, *Racially Separate or Together, op. cit.,* p. 246): "Relative deprivation for the white working-class Wallace supporters in Gary, however, derives largely from perceiving that groups regarded as lower in status and skills – especially black Americans – are unfairly gaining on their position."

16. For related and similar findings, see Jeffries, Turner, and Morris, *op. cit.,* p. 448; Campbell, *op. cit.,* p. 52; and H. Edward Ransford, "Blue Collar Anger: Reactions to Student and Black Protest," *American Sociological Review,* Volume 37 (June 1972), p. 339. See also Blumenthal et al., *op. cit.,* pp. 147-9.

17. Gus Tyler, "White Workers/Blue Mood," *Dissent,* (Winter 1972), p. 196.

18. The reaction to Lipset among social scientists has a fascinating history. The initial attempt to discredit Lipset focused upon proving that no differences – in authoritarianism – exist between the working class and the middle class. Later attempts to refute Lipset have centered on proving that a difference does exist between the working class and the middle class – and that the affluent working class retains its identity, and is no less liberal than the middle class. For examples of the latter reaction, see Richard F. Hamilton, *Affluence and the French Worker in the Fourth Republic* (Princeton: Princeton University Press, 1967), pp. 40-67; Richard F. Hamilton, "Affluence and the Worker: The West German Case," *American Journal of Sociology,* Volume 71 (September 1965), pp. 144-52; and John H. Goldthorpe, David Lockwood, Frank Bechhofer, and Jennifer Platt, *The Affluent Worker: Political Attitudes and Behavior* (Cambridge: Cambridge University Press, 1968). In addition, good general discussions of the "embourgeoisement" explanation can be found in James W. Rinehart, "Affluence and the Embourgeoisement of the Working Class: A Critical Look," *Social Problems,* Volume 19 (Fall 1971), pp. 149-62, and J.H. Westergaard, "The Withering Away of Class: A Contemporary Myth," in Perry Anderson and Robin Blackburn, (eds.), *Towards Socialism* (Ithaca: Cornell University Press, 1965), pp. 77-113.

19. Lewis Lipsitz, "Working-Class Authoritarianism: A Re-Evaluation," *American Sociological Review,* Volume 30 (February 1965), pp. 103-9. Morris Janowitz and Dwaine Marvick, in their "Authoritarianism and Political Behavior" (*Public Opinion Quarterly,* Volume 17 (Summer 1953), pp. 185-201), display findings which are contrary to those of Lipsitz.

20. Richard F. Hamilton, "Class and Race in the United States," in George Fischer, *op. cit.,* pp. 81-106. See also: Richard F. Hamilton, "The Marginal Middle Class: A Reconsideration," *American Sociological Review,* Volume 31 (April 1966), pp. 192-9; and Hamilton, "Blacks Demands, White Reactions, and Liberal Alarms," *op. cit.,* pp. 132-40.

21. For example, see S.M. Miller and Frank Riessman, " 'Working-Class Authoritarianism': A Critique of Lipset," *British Journal of Sociology,* Volume 12 (September 1961), pp. 263-81; and Frank Parkin, "Working-Class Conservatives: A Theory of Political Deviance," *British Journal of Sociology,* Volume 18 (September 1967), pp. 278-90.

Chapter 6

Conclusions

1. Anais Nin, *The Diary of Anais Nin: 1934-1939,* Volume Two, edited by

Gunther Stuhlmann (New York: Harcourt Brace Jovanovich, Inc., 1967), p. 146.

2. Engels to Friedrich Sorge, 29 November 1886, in Marx and Engels, *Selected Correspondence, op. cit.,* p. 451.

3. For example, see Kirkham, Levy, and Crotty, *op. cit.,* p. 213.

4. Wiatr, *op. cit.,* p. 28.

5. Thus, in proferring advice to Meyer and Vogt, German socialists who immigrated to the United States in the mid-1860's, Marx maintains that ethnic divisions within the American working class will impede the growth of subjective class consciousness. Marx to Meyer and Vogt, 9 April 1870, in Marx and Engels, *Letters to Americans, op. cit.,* pp. 77-80.

6. Marx and Engels, *The Communist Manifesto, op. cit.,* p. 24.

7. Georg Lukacs, "Class Consciousness," in Georg Lukacs, *History and Class Consciousness, op. cit.,* p. 66.

8. *Ibid.,* p. 58.

9. Pete Hamill, "The Revolt of the White Lower-Middle Class," in Louise Kapp Howe, (ed.), *The White Majority: Between Poverty and Affluence* (New York: Vintage Books, 1970), p. 15.

10. See Figure 5-4 in Chapter 5.

11. Pettigrew, *Racially Separate Or Together?, op. cit.,* p. 246. For an equally excellent explanation of this argument, see Vanneman and Pettigrew, *op. cit.* Lane also hypothesizes that "the greater the emphasis in a society upon equality of opportunity, the greater the tendency for those of marginal status to denigrate those lower than themselves" (Robert E. Lane, *Political Ideology: Why the American Common Man Believes What He Does* (New York: The Free Press of Glencoe 1962), p. 79).

12. Nisbet, "Has Futurology a Future?," *op. cit.,* p. 20.

13. I wish that this statement could be made more strongly. However, the differences between blue- and white-collar workers' perceptions of governmental acquiescence complicate the picture. Political discontents are more prevalent among blue-collar workers. However, blue-collar workers are also more likely to feel that the government will take harsh action to quell discontent. Despite their greater political dissatisfactions, they might not take revolutionary action because of their fear of governmental repression.

14. Again, the argument must be qualified. Murray Edelman (*The Symbolic Uses of Politics,* Urbana: University of Illinois Press, 1964) might argue that political power dissatisfactions will go the way of economic dissatisfactions. Through symbolic rewards, the government could defuse political power dissatisfactions without actually increasing the political power of blue-collar workers.

15. For a similar argument concerning economic inequality, see Lane, *op. cit.,* pp. 61-71, *passim.*

16. In otherwise excellent research, Centers, *op. cit.,* measures subjective

cognitive but not subjective affective class consciousness, while Leggett, *op. cit.,* constructs a multi-item index which includes questions tapping both subjective cognitive and subjective affective class consciousness.

17. As was noted earlier, Campbell and Schuman dissent from the Kerner Commission white racism explanation in their "Racial Attitudes in Fifteen American Cities," *op. cit.,* pp. 62-3.

18. See Myrdal, *op. cit.,* pp. 55-6; and Gouldner, *op. cit.,* pp. 488-90.

Appendix A

1. Campbell and Schuman, *op. cit.,* p. 58; Morris and Jeffries, *op. cit.,* p. 503.

2. David W. Abbott, Louis H. Gold, and Edward T. Rogowsky, *Police Politics and Race: The New York City Referendum on Civilian Review* (Cambridge: Joint Center for Urban Studies, 1969), p. 47.

3. H.J. Eysenck, "Social Attitudes and Social Class," *British Journal of Sociology,* Volume 1 (March 1950), pp. 57-8. Reprinted with permission of the London School of Economics and Routledge and Kegan Paul Ltd.

4. Abbott, Gold, and Rogowsky report a 56% response rate, including the easier to locate females (Abbott, Gold, and Rogowsky, *op. cit.,* p. 47). Campbell and Schuman report a 68% response rate for urban whites, also including females (Campbell and Schuman, *op. cit.,* p. 65). Interestingly, Campbell and Schuman indicate higher response rates for blacks than for urban whites; they also point out that the response rates for their 32 different samples varied over a range of 37 percentage points.

Bibliography

Abbott, David W.; Gold, Louis H.; and Rogowsky, Edward T. *Police Politics and Race: The New York City Referendum on Civilian Review.* Cambridge: The Joint Center for Urban Studies, 1969.

Aberbach, Joel D. "Alienation and Political Behavior," *American Political Science Review,* Volume 63 (March 1969), pp. 86-99.

———, and Walker, Jack L. "The Meanings of Black Power: A Comparison of White and Black Interpretations of a Political Slogan," *American Political Science Review,* Volume 64 (June 1970), pp. 367-88.

———. "Political Trust and Racial Ideology," *American Political Science Review,* Volume 64 (December 1970), pp. 1199-1219.

"The Agony of Busing Moves North," *Time,* 15 November 1971, pp. 57-64.

Arendt, Hannah. *On Violence.* New York: Harcourt, Brace and World, Inc., 1970.

Armor, David J. "The Evidence on Busing," *The Public Interest,* Number 28 (Summer 1972), pp. 90-126.

Ash, William. *Marxism and Moral Concepts.* New York: Monthly Review Press, 1964.

Avineri, Shlomo. *The Social and Political Thought of Karl Marx.* New York: Cambridge University Press, 1968.

Bandyopadhyay, Pradeep. "One Sociology or Many: Some Issues in Radical Sociology," *Science and Society,* Volume 35 (Spring 1971), pp. 1-26.

Banfield, Edward C. "Rioting Mainly for Fun and Profit." In Edward C. Banfield, *The Unheavenly City: The Nature and Future of Our Urban Crisis.* Boston: Little, Brown and Company, 1970, pp. 185-209.

Bayley, David H., and Mendelsohn, Harold. *Minorities and the Police: Confrontation in America.* New York: The Free Press, 1969.

Beardwood, Roger. "The New Negro Mood," *Fortune Magazine,* Volume 77 (January 1968), pp. 146-52.

Becker, John F., and Heaton, Eugene E. Jr. "The Election of Senator Edward R. Brooke," *Public Opinion Quarterly,* Volume 31 (Fall 1967), pp. 346-58.

Bell, Daniel. "The Dispossessed." In Daniel Bell, (ed.), *The Radical Right.* New York: Anchor Books, 1963, pp. 1-45.

———. "The 'Rediscovery' of Alienation: Some Notes Along the Quest for the Historical Marx," *Journal of Philosophy*, Volume 56 (November 1959), pp. 933-53.

Bendix, Reinhard. *Max Weber: An Intellectual Portrait.* Garden City: Doubleday and Company, Inc., 1962.

Bennett, Lerone, Jr. *Confrontation: Black and White.* Baltimore: Penguin Books, Inc., 1965.

Benoit-Smullyan, Emile. "Status, Status Types, and Status Interrelations," *American Sociological Review,* Volume 9 (April 1944), pp. 151-61.

Berkowitz, Leonard. "The Study of Urban Violence: Some Implications of Laboratory Studies of Frustration and Aggression." In Louis H. Masotti and Don R. Bowen, (eds.), *Riots and Rebellion: Civil Violence in the Urban Community.* Beverly Hills: Sage Publications, Inc., 1968, pp. 39-49.

Bienen, Henry. *Violence and Social Change: A Review of Current Literature.* Chicago: University of Chicago Press, 1968.

Binzen, Peter. *Whitetown, U.S.A.* New York: Random House, Inc., 1970.

Birnbaum, Norman. "The Crisis in Marxist Sociology." In Hans Peter Dreitzell, (ed.), *Recent Sociology,* No. 1. London: The Macmillan Company, 1969, pp. 12-42.

Blalock, Hubert M. Jr. *Toward A Theory of Minority-Group Relations.* New York: John Wiley and Sons, Inc., 1967.

Blauner, Robert. *Alienation and Freedom: The Factory Worker and His Industry.* Chicago: University of Chicago Press, 1964.

Bloombaum, Milton. "The Conditions Underlying Race Riots as Portrayed by Multidimensional Scalogram Analysis: A Reanalysis of Lieberson and Silverman's Data," *American Sociological Review,* Volume 33 (February 1968), pp. 76-91.

Blumenthal, Monica D.; Kahn, Robert L.; Andrews, Frank M.; and Head, Kendra B. *Justifying Violence: Attitudes of American Men.* Ann Arbor, Michigan: Institute for Social Research, 1972.

Bober, M. M. *Karl Marx's Interpretation of History,* Second Edition. New York: W. W. Norton and Company, 1948.

Boston Globe, 1965-72.

Bottomore, T. B. *Classes in Modern Society.* New York: Vintage Books, 1966.

Bowen, Don R.; Bowen, Elinor; Gawiser, Sheldon; and Masotti, Louis H. "Deprivation, Mobility, and Orientation Toward Protest of the Urban Poor." In Louis H. Masotti and Don R. Bowen, (eds.), *Riots and Rebellion: Civil Violence in the Urban Community.* Beverly Hills: Sage Publication, Inc., 1968, pp. 187-200.

Brink, William, and Harris, Louis. *Black and White: A Study of U.S. Racial Attitudes Today.* New York: Simon and Schuster, 1967.

_____. *The Negro Revolution in America.* New York: Simon and Schuster, 1963.

Brown, Richard Maxwell, (ed.). *American Violence.* Englewood Cliffs, N.J.: Prentice-Hall, Inc., 1970.

Campbell, Angus. *White Attitudes Toward Black People.* Ann Arbor, Michigan: Institute for Social Research, 1971.

_____, and Schuman, Howard. "Racial Attitudes in Fifteen American Cities." In *Supplemental Studies for the National Advisory Commission on Civil Disorders.* Washington, D.C.: U.S. Government Printing Office, 1968, pp. 1-67.

Cantril, Hadley. *The Pattern of Human Concerns.* New Brunswick: Rutgers University Press, 1965.

Caplan, Nathan. "The New Ghetto Man: A Review of Recent Empirical Studies," *Journal of Social Issues,* Volume 26 (Winter 1970), pp. 59-73.

_____, and Paige, Jeffrey M. "A Study of Ghetto Rioters," *Scientific American,* Volume 219 (August 1968), pp. 15-21.

Case, Herman M. "An Independent Test of the Interest-Group Theory of Social Class," *American Sociological Review,* Volume 17 (December 1952), pp. 751-5.

_____. "Marxian Implications of Centers' Interest-Group Theory: A Critical Appraisal," *Social Forces,* Volume 33 (March 1955), pp. 254-8.

Cataldo, Everett F.; Johnson, Richard M.; and Kellstadt, Lyman A. "Social Strain and Urban Violence." In Louis H. Masotti and Don R. Bowen, (eds.), *Riots and Rebellion: Civil Violence in the Urban Community.* Beverly Hills: Sage Publications, Inc., 1968, pp. 285-98.

Centers, Richard. *The Psychology of Social Classes.* Princeton: Princeton University Press, 1949.

Clark, Kenneth B. "Group Violence: A Preliminary Study of the Attitudinal Pattern of Its Acceptance and Rejection." In Allen D. Grimshaw, (ed.), *Racial Violence in the United States.* Chicago: Aldine Publishing Company, 1969, pp. 421-33.

Coles, Robert. *The Middle Americans.* Boston: Little, Brown and Company, 1971.

_____. "The Psychology of White Racists," *New York Review of Books,* Volume 17 (30 December 1971), pp. 12-5.

Conant, Ralph W.; Levy, Sheldon; and Lewis, Ralph. "Mass Polarization: Negro and White Attitudes on the Pace of Integration," *American Behavioral Scientist,* Volume 13 (November-December 1969), pp. 247-63.

Converse, Philip E. "The Nature of Belief Systems in Mass Publics." In David E. Apter, (ed.), *Ideology and Discontent.* New York: The Free Press, 1964, pp. 206-61.

_____; Miller, Warren E.; Rusk, Jerrold G.; and Wolfe, Arthur C. "Continuity and Change in American Politics: Parties and Issues in the 1968 Election," *American Political Science Review,* Volume 63 (December 1969), pp. 1083-1105.

_____, and Schuman, Howard. " 'Silent Majorities' and the Vietnam War," *Scientific American,* Volume 222 (June 1970), pp. 17-25.

Conway, M. Margaret. "The White Backlash Re-examined: Wallace and the 1964 Primaries," *Social Science Quarterly,* Volume 49 (December 1968), pp. 710-19.

Cook, Fred. "Hard-Hats: The Rampaging Patriots," *Nation,* 15 June 1970, pp. 712-9.

Coser, Lewis A. "Karl Marx and Contemporary Sociology." In Lewis A. Coser, *Continuities in the Study of Social Conflict.* New York: The Free Press, 1967, pp. 137-51.

Cox, Oliver. "Max Weber on Social Stratification: A Critique, " *American Sociological Review,* Volume 15 (April 1950), pp. 223-7.

Dahrendorf, Ralf. *Class and Class Conflict in Industrial Society.* Stanford: Stanford University Press, 1959.

Daly, Charles U., (ed.). *Urban Violence.* Chicago: University of Chicago Press, 1969.

Davies, James C. "Toward a Theory of Revolution," *American Sociological Review,* Volume 27 (February 1962), pp. 5-19.

———, (ed.). *When Men Revolt and Why: A Reader in Political Violence and Revolution.* New York: The Free Press, 1971.

Dean, Dwight G. "Alienation and Political Apathy," *Social Forces,* Volume 38 (March 1960), pp. 185-95.

———. "Alienation: Its Meaning and Measurement," *American Sociological Review,* Volume 26 (October 1961), pp. 753-8.

Demaris, Ovid. *America The Violent.* Baltimore: Penguin Books, Inc., 1970.

Denitch, Bogdan. "Is There A 'New Working Class'?", *Dissent,* (July-August 1970), pp. 351-5.

Downes, Bryan T. "Social and Political Characteristics of Riot Cities: A Comparative Study," *Social Science Quarterly,* Volume 49 (December 1968), pp. 504-20.

Drake, St. Clair. "Urban Violence and American Social Movements." In Robert H. Connery, (ed.), *Urban Riots: Violence and Social Change.* New York: Vintage Books, 1968, pp. 15-26.

Draper, Hal. "The Dictatorship of the Proletariat." In Michael Curtis, (ed.), *Marxism.* New York: Atherton Press, 1970, pp. 285-96.

Edelman, Murray. *The Symbolic Uses of Politics.* Urbana: University of Illinois Press, 1964.

Erskine, Hazel. "The Polls: Demonstrations and Race Riots," *Public Opinion Quarterly,* Volume 31 (Winter 1967-1968), pp. 655-77.

Eysenck, H.J. "Social Attitude and Social Class," *British Journal of Sociology,* Volume 1 (March 1950), pp. 56-66.

Fanon, Frantz. *The Wretched of the Earth.* New York: Grove Press, Inc., 1963.

Feagin, Joe R. and Sheatsley, Paul B. "Ghetto Resident Appraisals of a Riot," *Public Opinion Quarterly,* Volume 32 (Fall 1968), pp. 352-62.

Fetscher, Iring. "The Young and the Old Marx." In Nicholas Lobkowicz, (ed.), *Marx and the Western World*. Notre Dame: University of Notre Dame Press, 1967, pp. 19-39.

Feuer, Lewis S. "What Is Alienation: The Career of a Concept." In Lewis S. Feuer, *Marx and the Intellectuals: A Set of Post-Ideological Essays*. Garden City: Anchor Books, 1969, pp. 70-99.

Finifter, Ada W., (ed.). *Alienation and the Social System*. New York: John Wiley and Sons, Inc., 1972.

_____. "Dimensions of Political Alienation," *American Political Science Review*, Volume 64 (June 1970), pp. 389-410.

Fogelson, Robert M. *Violence As Protest: A Study of Riots and Ghettos*. Garden City, New York: Doubleday and Company, Inc., 1971.

_____; Black, Gordon S.; and Lipsky, Michael. "Review Symposium: Report of the National Advisory Commission on Civil Disorders and Supplemental Studies for the National Advisory Commission on Civil Disorders," *American Political Science Review*, Volume 63 (December 1969), pp. 1269-81.

Form, William, and Rytina, Joan H. "Ideological Beliefs on the Distribution of Power in the United States," *American Sociological Review*, Volume 34 (February 1969), pp. 19-31.

_____, and Pease, John. "Income and Stratification Ideology: Beliefs About the American Opportunity Structure," *American Journal of Sociology*, Volume 75 (January 1970), pp. 703-16.

Forward, John R., and Williams, Jay R. "Internal-External Control and Black Militancy," *Journal of Social Issues*, Volume 26 (Winter 1970), pp. 75-92.

Frady, Marshall. "Gary, Indiana," *Harper's*, Volume 239 (August 1969), pp. 35-45.

Freire, Paulo. *Pedagogy of the Oppressed*. Translated by Myra Bergman Ramos. New York: Herder and Herder, 1970.

Fromm, Erich. *Marx's Concept of Man*. New York: Frederick Ungar Publishing Co., 1966.

Gamson, William A. *Power and Discontent*. Homewood, Ill.: The Dorsey Press, 1968.

_____, and McEvoy, James. "Police Violence and Its Public Support." In James F. Short, Jr., and Marvin E. Wolfgang, (eds.), *Collective Violence*. Chicago: Aldine-Atherton, Inc., 1972, pp. 329-42.

Geschwender, James A. "Civil Rights Protest and Riots: A Disappearing Distinction," *Social Science Quarterly*, Volume 49 (December 1968), pp. 474-84.

_____. "Social Structure and the Negro Revolt: An Examination of Some Hypotheses," *Social Forces*, Volume 43 (December 1964), pp. 248-56.

Glantz, Oscar. "Class Consciousness and Political Solidarity," *American Sociological Review*, Volume 23 (August 1958), pp. 375-83.

Glazer, Nathan. "Blacks and Ethnic Groups: The Difference, and the Political Difference It Makes," *Social Problems,* Volume 18 (Spring 1971), pp. 444-61.

Glenn, Norval D. "Occupational Benefits to Whites from Subordination of Negroes," *American Sociological Reveiw,* Volume 28 (June 1963), pp. 443-8.

_____. "The Role of White Resistance and Facilitation in the Negro Struggle for Equality," *Phylon,* Volume 26 (Summer 1965), pp. 105-16.

_____. "White Gains from Negro Subordination," *Social Problems,* Volume 14 (Fall 1966), pp. 159-78.

Goffman, Irving W. "Status Consistency and Preference for Change in Power Distribution," *American Sociological Review,* Volume 22 (June 1957), pp. 275-81.

Goldschmid, Marcel L., (ed.). *Black Americans and White Racism: Theory and Research.* New York: Holt, Rinehart and Winston, Inc., 1970.

Goldthorpe, John H.; Lockwood, David; Benchhofer, Frank; and Platt, Jennifer. *The Affluent Worker in the Class Structure.* Cambridge: Cambridge University Press, 1969.

_____. *The Affluent Worker: Political Attitudes and Behavior.* Cambridge: Cambridge University Press, 1968.

Goodman, Paul. "Reflections on Racism, Spite, Guilt, and Violence," *New York Review of Books,* 23 May 1968, pp. 18-23.

Gordon, Milton M. *Social Class in American Sociology.* New York: McGraw-Hill Book Company, 1958.

Gouldner, Alvin W. *The Coming Crisis of Western Sociology.* New York: Basic Books, 1970.

Gourevitch, Peter. "Anatomy of 'Affluent Workers,' " *Dissent,* (February 1971), pp. 86-90.

Greeley, Andrew M. "Political Attitudes Among American White Ethnics," *Public Opinion Quarterly,* Volume 36 (Summer 1972), pp. 213-20.

_____. *That Most Distressful Nation: The Taming of the American Irish.* Chicago: Quadrangle Books, 1972.

_____, and Sheatsley, Paul B. "Attitudes Toward Racial Integration," *Scientific American,* Volume 225 (December 1971), pp. 13-9.

Grimshaw, Allen D. "Actions of Police and Military in American Race Riots," *Phylon,* Volume 24 (Fall 1963), pp. 271-89.

_____. "Factors Contributing to Colour Violence in the United States and Great Britain," *Race,* Volume 5 (May 1962), pp. 3-19.

_____. "Interpreting Collective Violence: An Argument for the Importance of Social Structure." In James F. Short, Jr., and Marvin E. Wolfgang, (eds.), *Collective Violence.* Chicago: Aldine-Atherton, Inc., 1972, pp. 35-46.

_____. "Three Views of Urban Violence: Civil Disturbance, Racial Revolt, Class Assault." In Allen D. Grimshaw, (ed.), *Racial Violence in the United States.* Chicago: Aldine Publishing Company, 1969, pp. 385-96.

———. "Urban Racial Violence in the United States: Changing Ecological Considerations," *American Journal of Sociology,* Volume 64 (September 1960), pp. 109-19.

Gross, Llewellyn. "The Use of Class Concepts in Sociological Research," *American Journal of Sociology,* Volume 54 (January 1949), pp. 409-21.

Gross, Neal. "Social Class Identification in the Urban Community," *American Sociological Review,* Volume 18 (August 1953), pp. 398-404.

Gurr, Ted Robert. "A Comparative Study of Civil Strife." In Hugh Davis Graham and Ted Robert Gurr, (eds.), *Violence in America: Historical and Comparative Perspectives.* New York: Bantam Books, 1969, pp. 572-632.

———. "Urban Disorder: Perspectives from the Comparative Study of Civil Strife." In Louis H. Masotti and Don R. Bowen, (eds.), *Riots and Rebellion: Civil Violence in the Urban Community.* Beverly Hills: Sage Publications, Inc., 1968, pp. 51-67.

———. *Why Men Rebel.* Princeton: Princeton University Press, 1970.

Haer, John L. "An Empirical Study of Social Class Awareness," *Social Forces,* Volume 36 (December 1957), pp. 117-21.

Hahn, Harlan D. "Civic Responses to Riots: A Reappraisal of Kerner Commission Data," *Public Opinion Quarterly,* Volume 34, (Spring 1970), pp. 101-7.

———. "Correlates of Public Sentiment About War: Local Referenda on the Vietnam Issue," *American Political Science Review,* Volume 69 (December 1970), pp. 1186-98.

———. "Ghetto Sentiments on Violence," *Science and Society,* Volume 33 (Spring 1969), pp. 197-208.

———. "The Political Objectives of Ghetto Violence." Paper delivered at 1969 Meetings of the American Political Science Association.

Hamill, Pete. "The Revolt of the White Lower-Middle Class." In Louise Kapp Howe, (ed.), *The White Majority: Between Poverty and Affluence.* New York: Vintage Books, 1970, pp. 10-22.

Hamilton, Richard F. *Affluence and the French Worker in the Fourth Republic.* Princeton: Princeton University Press, 1967.

———. "Affluence and the Worker: The West German Case," *American Journal of Sociology,* Volume 71 (September 1965), pp. 144-52.

———. "Black Demands, White Reactions, and Liberal Alarms." In Sar A. Levitan, (ed.), *Blue-Collar Workers: A Symposium on Middle America.* New York: McGraw-Hill Book Company, 1971, pp. 130-53.

———. "Class and Race in the United States," in George Fischer, (ed.), *The Revival of American Socialism.* New York: Oxford University Press, 1971, pp. 81-106.

———. "Income, Class, and Reference Groups," *American Sociological Review,* Volume 29 (August 1964), pp. 576-9.

———. "Liberal Intelligentsia and White Backlash," *Dissent,* (Winter 1972), pp. 225-32.

——. "The Marginal Middle Class: A Reconsideration," *American Sociological Review,* Volume 31 (April 1966), pp. 192-200.

——. "Reply to Tucker," *American Sociological Review,* Volume 31 (December 1966), pp. 856.

——. "Skill Level and Politics," *Public Opinion Quarterly,* Volume 29 (Fall 1965), pp. 390-9.

Handlin, Oscar. *Boston's Immigrants: A Study in Acculturation,* revised and enlarged edition. New York: Atheneum, 1959.

Hatt, Paul K. "Stratification in the Mass Society," *American Sociological Review,* Volume 15 (April 1950), pp. 216-22.

Hazelrigg, Lawrence E. "Class, Property, and Authority: Dahrendorf's Critique of Marx's Theory of Class," *Social Forces,* Volume 50 (June 1972), pp. 473-87.

Hetzler, Stanley Arthur. "An Investigation of the Distinctiveness of Social Classes," *American Sociological Review,* Volume 18 (October 1953), pp. 493-7.

Hodges, Donald Clark. "Old and New Working Classes," *Radical America,* Volume 5 (January-February 1971), pp. 11-32.

——. "The Unity of Marx's Thought." In Michael Curtis, (ed.), *Marxism.* New York: Atherton Press, 1970, pp. 39-45.

Hofstadter, Richard, and Wallace, Michael, (eds.). *American Violence: A Documentary History.* New York: Alfred A. Knopf, 1970.

Hughes, H. Stuart. *Consciousness and Society: The Reorientation of European Social Thought, 1890-1930.* New York: Vintage Books, 1958.

Hunt, R.N. Carew. "The Ethics of Marxism." In Michael Curtis, (ed.), *Marxism.* New York: Atherton Press, 1970, pp. 109-17.

Huthmacher, J. Joseph. *Massachusetts People and Politics: 1919-1933.* New York: Atheneum, 1959.

Hyman, Herbert H., and Sheatsley, Paul B. "Attitudes Toward Desegregation," *Scientific American,* Volume 195 (December 1956), pp. 35-9.

——. "Attitudes Toward Desegregation," *Scientific American,* Volume 211 (July 1964), pp. 16-23.

Hyman, Martin D. "Determining the Effects of Status Inconsistency," *Public Opinion Quarterly,* Volume 30 (Spring 1966), pp. 120-9.

Janowitz, Morris. "Patterns of Collective Racial Violence." In Hugh Davis Graham and Ted Robert Gurr, (eds.), *Violence in America: Historical and Comparative Perspectives.* New York: Bantam Books, 1969, pp. 418-29.

——, and Marvick, Dwaine. "Authoritarianism and Political Behavior," *Public Opinion Quarterly,* Volume 17 (Summer 1953), pp. 185-201.

Jeffries, Vincent; Turner, Ralph H.; and Morris, Richard T. "The Public Perception of the Watts Riot as Social Protest," *American Sociological Review,* Volume 36 (June 1971), pp. 443-51.

Kahl, Joseph. *The American Class Structure.* New York: Rinehart and Company, Inc., 1957.

———, and Davis, James A. "A Comparison of Indexes of Socio-Economic Status," *American Sociological Review,* Volume 20 (June 1955), pp. 317-25.

Kamenka, Eugene. *The Ethical Foundations of Marxism.* New York: Frederick A. Praeger, Publisher, 1962.

———. "The Primitive Ethic of Karl Marx." In Michael Curtis, (ed.), *Marxism.* New York: Atherton Press, 1970, pp. 118-28.

Kautsky, Karl, *The Dictatorship of the Proletariat.* Ann Arbor: University of Michigan Press, 1964.

Kelly, K. Dennis, and Chambliss, William J. "Status Consistency and Political Attitudes," *American Sociological Review,* Volume 31 (June 1966), pp. 375-82.

Kenkel, William F. "The Relationship Between Status Consistency and Politico-economic Attitudes," *American Sociological Review,* Volume 21 (June 1956), pp. 365-8.

Kim, Young C. "Authority: Some Conceptual and Empirical Notes," *Western Political Quarterly,* Volume 19 (June 1966), pp. 223-34.

Kirkham, James F.; Levy, Sheldon; and Crotty, William J. *Assassination and Political Violence: A Report to the National Commission on the Causes and Prevention of Violence.* Washington, D.C.: U.S. Government Printing Office, 1969.

Kornhauser, William. *The Politics of Mass Society.* New York: The Free Press, 1959.

Kovel, Joel. *White Racism: A Psychohistory.* New York: Random House, Inc., 1970.

Landecker, Werner S. "Class Crystallization and Class Consciousness," *American Sociological Review,* Volume 28 (April 1963), pp. 219-29.

Lane, Robert E. *Political Ideology: Why the American Common Man Believes What He Does.* New York: The Free Press of Glencoe, 1962.

———, and Lerner, Michael. "Why Hard-Hats Hate Hairs," *Psychology Today,* (November 1970), pp. 45-8, 104-5.

Leggett, John C. *Class, Race, and Labor: Working-Class Consciousness in Detroit.* New York: Oxford University Press, 1968.

Lemon, Richard. *The Troubled American.* New York: Simon and Schuster, 1970.

Lenin, N. *The Proletarian Revolution and Kautsky the Renegade.* Detroit: Marxian Educational Society, no date.

Lenski, Gerhard E. "American Social Classes, Statistical Strata or Social Groups," *American Journal of Sociology,* Volume 58 (September 1952), pp. 139-44.

———. "Comment," *Public Opinion Quarterly,* Volume 28 (Summer 1964), pp. 326-30.

_____. "Social Participation and Status Crystallization," *American Sociological Review,* Volume 21 (August 1956), pp. 458-64.

_____. "Status Crystallization: A Non-Vertical Dimension of Social Status," *American Sociological Review,* Volume 19 (August 1954), pp. 405-13.

_____. "Status Inconsistency and the Vote: A Four Nation Test," *American Sociological Review,* Volume 32 (April 1967), pp. 298-301.

Levine, Robert A. "The Silent Majority: Neither Simple Nor Simple-Minded," *Public Opinion Quarterly,* Volume 35 (Winter 1971-1972), pp. 571-7.

Levy, Frank. *Northern Schools and Civil Rights: The Racial Imbalance Act of Massachusetts.* Chicago: Markham Publishing Company, 1971.

Levy, Sheldon G. "Polarization in Racial Attitudes," *Public Opinion Quarterly,* Volume 36 (Summer 1972), pp. 221-34.

_____. "The Psychology of Political Activity." In James F. Short, Jr., and Marvin E. Wolfgang, (eds.), *Collective Violence.* Chicago: Aldine-Atherton, Inc., 1972, pp. 210-23.

_____. "The Psychology of the Politically Violent." Paper delivered at the 1969 Meetings of the Pacific Sociology Association.

_____. "Response Orientation to Governmental Injustice." Paper delivered at the 1969 Meetings of the Midwest Psychology Association.

_____. "Special Research Report." In Sheldon G. Levy, James F. Kirkham, and William J. Crotty, *Assassination and Political Violence: A Staff Report to the National Commission on the Causes and Prevention of Violence.* Washington, D.C.: U.S. Government Printing Office, 1969, pp. 383-417.

Lichtheim, George. *Marxism: An Historical and Critical Survey.* New York: Frederick A. Praeger, Inc. 1964.

Lieberson, Stanley, and Silverman, Arnold R. "The Precipitants and Underlying Conditions of Race Riots," *American Sociological Review,* Volume 30 (December 1965), pp. 887-98.

Lipset, Seymour M. *The First New Nation: The United States in Historical and Comparative Perspective.* New York: Anchor Books, 1963.

_____. "Is Gradual Change Possible?" In Michael Curtis, (ed.), *Marxism.* New York: Atherton Press, 1970, pp. 275-9.

_____. "Issues in Social Class Analysis." In Seymour Martin Lipset, *Revolution and Counter-revolution: Change and Persistence in Social Structures,* revised edition. New York: Anchor Books, 1970, pp. 157-201.

_____. *Political Man: The Social Bases of Politics.* New York: Anchor Books, 1960.

_____. "The Sources of the 'Radical Right.' " In Daniel Bell, (ed.), *The Radical Right.* New York: Anchor Books, 1963, pp. 307-71.

_____, and Bendix, Reinhard. "Karl Marx's Theory of Social Classes." In Seymour Martin Lipset and Reinhard Bendix, (eds.), *Class, Status, and Power:*

Social Stratification in Comparative Perspective, Second Edition. New York: The Free Press, 1966, pp. 6-11.

——, and Raab, Earl. *The Politics of Unreason: Right-Wing Extremism in America, 1790-1970.* New York: Harper and Row, Publishers, 1970.

Lipsitz, Lewis. "Work Life and Political Attitudes: A Study of Manual Workers," *American Political Science Review,* Volume 58 (December 1964), pp. 951-62.

——. "Working Class Authoritarianism: A Re-evaluation," *American Sociological Review,* Volume 30 (February 1965), pp. 103-9.

Lipsky, Michael, "Protest As A Political Resource," *American Political Science Review,* Volume 62 (December 1968), pp. 1144-58.

——, and Olson, David J. "On the Politics of Riot Commissions." Paper delivered at the 1968 Meetings of the American Political Science Association.

Litt, Edgar. *The Political Cultures of Massachusetts.* Cambridge: The MIT Press, 1965.

——. "Political Cynicism and Political Futility," *Journal of Politics,* Volume 25 (May 1963), pp. 312-23.

Lockwood, David. *The Blackcoated Worker: A Study in Class Consciousness.* London: Unwin University Books, 1958.

Lukacs, Georg. *History and Class Consciousness: Studies in Marxist Dialectics.* Translated by Rodney Livingstone. Cambridge: The MIT Press, 1971.

Lupsha, Peter A. "On Theories of Urban Violence." Paper delivered at the 1968 Meetings of the American Political Science Association.

McDill, Edward L., and Ridley, Jeanne Clare. "Status, Anomia, Political Alienation, and Political Participation," *American Journal of Sociology,* Volume 68 (September 1962), pp. 205-13.

McGovern, Arthur F. "The Young Marx on the State," *Science and Society,* Volume 34 (Winter 1970), pp. 430-66.

McPhail, Clark. "Civil Disorder Participation: A Critical Examination of Recent Research," *American Sociological Review,* Volume 36 (December 1971), pp. 1058-73.

Manis, Jerome G., and Meltzer, Bernard N. "Attitudes of Textile Workers to Class Structure," *American Journal of Sociology,* Volume 60 (July 1954), pp. 30-5.

——. "Some Correlates of Class Consciousness Among Textile Workers," *American Journal of Sociology,* Volume 69 (September 1963), pp. 177-84.

Marcuse, Herbert. *Soviet Marxism: A Critical Analysis.* New York: Vintage Books, 1961.

Marshall, Ray. "Black Workers and the Unions," *Dissent,* (Winter 1972), pp. 295-302.

Marx, Gary T. "Issueless Riots." In James F. Short, Jr., and Marvin E. Wolfgang, (eds.), *Collective Violence.* Chicago: Aldine-Atherton, Inc., 1972, pp. 47-59.

_____. *Protest and Prejudice: A Study of Belief in the Black Community*. New York: Harper and Row, Publishers, 1969.

_____. "Report of the National Commission: The Analysis of Disorder or Disorderly Analysis?" Paper delivered at the 1968 Meetings of the American Political Science Association.

Marx, Karl. *Capital: A Critique of Political Economy,* 3 volumes. Edited by Frederick Engels, and translated by Samuel Moore and Edward Aveling. New York: International Publishers, 1967.

_____. *The Civil War in France*. New York: International Publishers, 1968.

_____. *Class Struggles in France: 1848-1850*. New York: International Publishers, 1964.

_____. *Critique of the Gotha Programme*. New York: International Publishers, 1966.

_____. *The Economic and Philosophic Manuscripts of 1844*. Edited by Dirk J. Struik and translated by Martin Milligan. New York: International Publishers, 1964.

_____. *The Eighteenth Brumaire of Louis Bonaparte*. New York: International Publishers, 1963.

_____. *The Grundrisse*. Edited and translated by David McLellan. New York: Harper and Row, Publishers, 1971.

_____. *Karl Marx: Early Writings*. Edited and translated by T.B. Bottomore. New York: McGraw-Hill Book Company, 1963.

_____. *Karl Marx: Selected Writings in Sociology and Social Philosophy*. Edited by T.B. Bottomore. New York: McGraw-Hill Book Company, 1956.

_____. *The Poverty of Philosophy*. New York: International Publishers, 1963.

_____. *Pre-Capitalist Economic Formations*. Edited by Eric J. Hobsbawm, and translated by Jack Cohen. New York: International Publishers, 1964.

_____. *Revolution and Counter-Revolution*. Edited by Eleanor Marx Aveling. New York: Capricorn Books, 1956.

_____. *Secret Diplomatic History of the Eighteenth Century and The Story of the Life of Lord Palmerston*. New York: International Publishers, 1969.

_____. "Theses on Feuerbach." In Lewis S. Feuer, (ed.), *Marx and Engels: Basic Writings on Politics and Philosophy*. Garden City: Doubleday and Company, Inc., 1959, pp. 243-5.

_____. *Wage-Labour and Capital*. New York: International Publishers, 1933.

_____, and Engels, Friedrich. *The Communist Manifesto*. New York: Monthly Review Press, 1964.

_____. *The German Ideology, Parts I and III*. New York: International Publishers, 1947.

———. *Letters to Americans, 1848-1895: A Selection.* Edited by Arthur Trachtenberg. New York: International Publishers, 1953.

———. *The Selected Correspondence of Karl Marx and Frederick Engels: 1846-1895.* New York: International Publishers, 1942.

Masotti, Louis H.; Hadden, Jeffrey K.; Seminatore, Kenneth F; and Corsi, Jerome R. *A Time To Burn: An Evaluation of the Present Crisis in Race Relations.* Chicago: Rand McNally and Company, 1969.

Matthews, Donald R., and Prothro, James W. *Negroes and the New Southern Politics.* New York: Harcourt, Brace and World, Inc., 1966.

Mayer, Kurt B., and Buckley, Walter. *Class and Society,* Third Edition. New York: Random House, 1970.

Merleau-Ponty, Maurice. *Humanism and Terror: An Essay on the Communist Problem.* Translated by John O'Neill. Boston: Beacon Press, 1969.

Metzger, L. Paul. "American Sociology and Black Assimilation: Conflicting Perspectives," *American Journal of Sociology,* Volume 76 (January 1971), pp. 627-47.

Meyer, John W., and Hammond, Phillip E. "Forms of Status Inconsistency," *Social Forces,* Volume 50 (September 1971), pp. 91-101.

Meyer, Philip. "Aftermath of Martyrdom: Negro Militancy and Martin Luther King," *Public Opinion Quarterly,* Volume 33 (Summer 1969), pp. 160-73.

Miller, Herman P. *Rich Man, Poor Man.* New York: Thomas Y. Crowell and Company, 1971.

Miller, S.M., and Riessman, Frank. " 'Working Class Authoritarianism': A Critique of Lipset," *British Journal of Sociology,* Volume 12 (September 1961), pp. 263-81.

Mills, C. Wright. *The Marxists.* New York: Dell Publishing Co., 1962.

Mitchell, Robert E. "Methodological Notes on a Theory of Status Crystallization," *Public Opinion Quarterly,* Volume 28 (Summer 1964), pp. 315-25.

Moore, Barrington, Jr. *Social Origins of Dictatorship and Democracy: Lord and Peasant in the Making of the Modern World.* Boston: Beacon Press, 1966.

Moore, Charles H. "The Politics of Urban Violence: Policy Outcomes in Winston-Salem, North Carolina." Paper presented at the 1969 Meetings of the American Political Science Association.

Morris, Richard T., and Jeffries, Vincent. "The White Reaction Study." In Nathan Cohen, (ed.), *The Los Angeles Riots: A Socio-Psychological Study.* New York: Praeger Publishers, 1970, pp. 480-601.

Murphy, Raymond J., and Watson, James M. "The Structure of Discontent: The Relationship Between Social Structure, Grievance, and Riot Support." In

Nathan Cohen, (ed.), *The Los Angeles Riots: A Socio-Psychological Study.* New York: Praeger Publishers, 1970, pp. 140-257.

Myrdal, Gunnar. *Objectivity in Social Research.* New York: Pantheon Books, 1969.

Neal, Arthur G., and Rettig, Saloman. "Dimensions of Alienation Among Manual and Non-Manual Workers," *American Sociological Review,* Volume 28 (August 1963), pp. 599-608.

____. "On the Multidimensionality of Alienation," *American Sociological Review,* Volume 32 (February 1967), pp. 54-64.

Nettler, Gwynn. "A Measure of Alienation," *American Sociological Review,* Volume 22 (December 1957), pp. 670-7.

New York Times, 1965-72.

Nicolaus, Martin. "The Crisis of Late Capitalism." In George Fischer, (ed.), *The Revival of American Socialism: Selected Papers of the Socialist Scholars Conference.* New York: Oxford University Press, 1971, pp. 3-21.

____. "Proletariat and Middle Class in Marx: Hegelian Choreography and the Capitalist Dialectic." In James Weinstein and David W. Eakins, (eds.), *For a New America: Essays in History and Politics from "Studies on the Left," 1959-1967.* New York: Vintage Books, 1970, pp. 253-83.

____. "The Unknown Marx." In Carl Oglesby, (ed.), *The New Left Reader.* New York: Grove Press, Inc., 1969, pp. 84-110.

Nieburg, H.L. *Political Violence: The Behavioral Process.* New York: St. Martin's Press, 1969.

Nisbet, Robert A. "The Decline and Fall of Social Class." In Robert A. Nisbet, *Tradition and Revolt: Historical and Sociological Essays.* New York: Vintage Books, 1966, pp. 105-27.

____. "Has Futurology a Future?," *Encounter* (November 1971), pp. 18-28.

Noel, Donald L. and Pinkney, Alphonso. "Correlates of Prejudice: Some Racial Differences and Similarities," *American Journal of Sociology,* Volume 69 (May 1964), pp. 609-22.

Novak, Michael. *The Rise of the Unmeltable Ethnics: Politics and Culture in the Seventies.* New York: The Macmillan Company, 1972.

Ollman, Bertell. *Alienation: Marx's Conception of Man in Capitalist Society.* New York: Cambridge University Press, 1971.

____. "Marx's Use of 'Class,' " *American Journal of Sociology,* Volume 73 (March 1968), pp. 573-80.

Olsen, Marvin E. "Alienation and Political Opinions," *Public Opinion Quarterly,* Volume 29 (Summer 1965), pp. 200-12.

____. "Perceived Legitimacy of Social Protest Actions," *Social Problems,* Volume 15 (Winter 1968), pp. 297-310.

Orum, Anthony M., and Orum, Amy W. "The Class and Status Bases of Negro Student Protest," *Social Science Quarterly,* Volume 49 (December 1968), pp. 521-33.

Ossowski, Stanislaw. *Class Structure in the Social Consciousness.* Translated by Sheila Patterson. New York: The Free Press, 1963.

Paige, Jeffrey M. "Political Orientation and Riot Participation," *American Sociological Review,* Volume 36 (October 1971), pp. 810-20.

Pappenheim, Fritz. *The Alienation of Modern Man: An Interpretation Based on Marx and Tonnies.* New York: Monthly Review Press, 1959.

Parkin, Frank. "Working Class Conservatives: A Theory of Political Deviance," *British Journal of Sociology,* Volume 18 (September 1967), pp. 278-90.

Pease, John; Form, William; and Rytina, Joan H. "Ideological Currents in American Stratification Literature," *American Sociologist,* Volume 5 (May 1970), pp. 127-37.

Pettigrew, Thomas F. "Racially Separate Or Together?," *Journal of Social Issues,* Volume 25 (January 1969), pp. 43-69.

_____. *Racially Separate Or Together?* New York: McGraw-Hill Book Company, 1971.

_____. "Social Evaluation Theory: Convergences and Applications." In David Levine, (ed.), *Nebraska Symposium on Motivation, 1967.* Lincoln: University of Nebraska Press, 1967, pp. 241-311.

_____, and Vanneman, Reeve D. "Race and Relative Deprivation in the Urban United States," *Race,* Volume 13 (April 1972), pp. 461-86.

Pinkney, Alphonso. *The American Way of Violence.* New York: Random House, Inc., 1972.

Platt, Anthony M., (ed.). *The Politics of Riot Commissions: 1917-1970.* New York: Collier Books, 1971.

Portes, Alejandro. "On The Interpretation of Class Consciousness," *American Journal of Sociology,* Volume 77 (September 1971), pp. 228-44.

Potter, David M. *People of Plenty: Economic Abundance and the American Character.* Chicago: University of Chicago Press, 1954.

Prothro, James W., and Grigg, Charles M. "Fundamental Principles of Democracy: Bases of Agreement and Disagreement," *Journal of Politics,* Volume 22 (May 1960), pp. 276-94.

Raine, Walter J. "The Ghetto Merchant Study." In Nathan Cohen, (ed.), *The Los Angeles Riots: A Socio-Psychological Study.* New York: Praeger Publishers, 1970, pp. 602-37.

_____. "The Perception of Police Brutality in South Central Los Angeles." In Nathan Cohen, (ed.), *The Los Angeles Riots: A Socio-Psychological Study.* New York: Praeger Publishers, 1970, pp. 380-412.

Ransford, H. Edward. "Blue Collar Anger: Reactions to Student and Black Protest," *American Sociological Review,* Volume 37 (June 1972), pp. 333-46.

_____. "Isolation, Powerlessness, and Violence: A Study of Attitudes and Participation in the Watts Riot," *American Journal of Sociology,* Volume 73 (March 1968), pp. 581-91.

Reiter, Howard L. "Blue-Collar Workers and the Future of American Politics." In Sar A. Levitan, (ed.), *Blue-Collar Workers: A Symposium on Middle America.* New York: McGraw-Hill Book Company, 1971, pp. 101-29.

"Report from Black America," *Newsweek,* (30 June 1969), pp. 17-35.

Report of the National Advisory Commission on Civil Disorders. Washington, D.C.: U.S. Government Printing Office, 1968.

Rice, Berkeley. "Boston — 'I Am a Symbol of Resistance' — Hicks," *New York Times Magazine* (5 November 1967).

Rinehart, James W. "Affluence and the Embourgeoisement of the Working Class: A Critical Look," *Social Problems,* Volume 19 (Fall 1971), pp. 149-62.

Robinson, John P. "Public Reaction to Political Protest: Chicago, 1968," *Public Opinion Quarterly,* Volume 34 (Spring 1970), pp. 1-9.

Rogin, Michael. "Wallace and the Middle Class: The White Backlash in Wisconsin," *Public Opinion Quarterly,* Volume 30 (Spring 1966), pp. 98-108.

Rogin, Richard. "Joe Kelly Has Reached His Boiling Point." In Murray Friedman, (ed.), *Overcoming Middle Class Rage.* Philadelphia: The Westminster Press, 1971, pp. 66-85.

Rokeach, Milton. *The Open and Closed Mind: Investigations Into the Nature of Belief Systems and Personality Systems.* New York: Basic Books, Inc., 1960.

Rose, Thomas, (ed.). *Violence in America: A Historical and Contemporary Reader.* New York: Vintage Books, 1969.

Rosenberg, Harold. "The Proletariat and the Revolution." In Michael Curtis, (ed.), *Marxism.* New York: Atherton Press, 1970, pp. 265-74.

Rossi, Peter H., (ed.). *Ghetto Revolts.* Chicago: Aldine Publishing Company, 1970.

Roth, Guenther. "Political Critiques of Max Weber: Some Implications for Political Sociology," *American Sociological Review,* Volume 30 (April 1965), pp. 213-23.

Runciman, W.G. *Relative Deprivation and Social Justice: A Study of Attitudes to Social Inequality in Twentieth Century England.* Berkeley and Los Angeles: University of California Press, 1966.

Rush, Gary B. "Status Consistency and Right-Wing Extremism," *American Sociological Review,* Volume 32 (February 1967), pp. 86-92.

Schlesinger, Arthur, Jr. *Violence: America in the Sixties.* New York: The New American Library, Inc., 1968.

Schoenberger, Robert A., and Segal, David R. "The Ecology of Dissent: The Southern Wallace Vote in 1968," *Midwest Journal of Political Science,* Volume 15 (August 1971), pp. 583-6.

Schrag, Peter. "The Decline of the WASP," *Harper's,* Volume 240 (April 1970), pp. 85-91.

_____. "The Forgotten American," *Harper's,* Volume 239 (August 1969), pp. 27-34.

_____. *Village School Downtown: Boston Schools, Boston Politics.* Boston: Beacon Press, 1967.

Schulman, Jay. "Ghetto-Area Residence, Political Alienation, and Riot Orientation." In Louis H. Masotti and Don R. Bowen, (eds.), *Riots and Rebellion: Civil Violence in the Urban Community.* Beverly Hills: Sage Publications, 1968, pp. 261-84.

Schwartz, Barry N., and Disch, Robert, (eds.). *White Racism: Its History, Pathology, and Practice.* New York: Dell Publishing Co., Inc., 1970.

Schwartz, David C. "Psychological Correlates of Urban Political Alienation: An Extension of Simulation Results Via Sample Interview Survey," *Western Political Quarterly,* Volume 23 (September 1970), pp. 600-10.

_____. "A Theory of Revolutionary Behavior." In James C. Davies, (ed.), *When Men Revolt and Why: A Reader in Political Violence and Revolution.* New York: The Free Press, 1971, pp. 109-32.

_____. "Urban Political Alienation: Ethnic Differences and Violent Consequences." Paper delivered at 1969 Meetings of the American Political Science Association.

_____, and Shubs, Peter. "From Political Alienation to Revolutionary Support." Paper delivered at 1968 Meetings of the Western Psychological Association.

Sears, David O. "Black Attitudes Toward the Political System in the Aftermath of the Watts Insurrection," *Midwest Journal of Political Science,* Volume 13 (November 1969), pp. 515-44.

_____. "Political Attitudes of Los Angeles Negroes." In Nathan Cohen, (ed.), *The Los Angeles Riots: A Socio-Psychological Study.* New York: Praeger Publishers, 1970, pp. 676-705.

_____, and McConahay, John B. "Participation in the Los Angeles Riot," *Social Problems,* Volume 17 (Summer 1969), pp. 3-20.

_____. "The Politics of Discontent." In Nathan Cohen, (ed.), *The Los Angeles Riots: A Socio-Psychological Study.* New York: Praeger Publishers, 1970, pp. 413-79.

_____. "Racial Socialization, Comparison Levels, and the Watts Riot," *Journal of Social Issues,* Volume 26 (Winter 1970), pp. 121-40.

Seeman, Melvin. "On the Meaning of Alienation," *American Sociological Review,* Volume 24 (December 1959), pp. 783-91.

Segal, David R. "Partisan Realignment in the United States: The Lesson of the 1964 Election," *Public Opinion Quarterly,* Volume 32 (Fall 1968), pp. 441-4.

_____. "Status Inconsistency, Cross Pressures, and American Political Behavior," *American Sociological Review,* Volume 34 (June 1969), pp. 352-9.

_____, and Knoke, David. "Social Mobility, Status Inconsistency and Partisan Realignment in the United States," *Social Forces,* Volume 47 (December 1968), pp. 154-8.

Sheatsley, Paul B. "White Attitudes Toward the Negro," *Daedalus,* Volume 95 (Winter 1966), pp. 217-38.

Silver, Allan A. "Official Interpretations of Racial Riots." In Robert H. Connery, (ed.), *Urban Riots: Violence and Social Change.* New York: Vintage Books, 1968, pp. 151-63.

Singer, Benjamin D.; Osborn, Richard W.; and Geschwender, James A. *Black Rioters: A Study of Social Factors and Communication in the Detroit Riot.* Lexington, Mass.: D.C. Heath and Company, 1970.

Skolnick, Jerome H. *The Politics of Protest.* New York: Ballantine Books, 1969.

Smelser, Neil J. *Theory of Collective Behavior.* New York: The Free Press, 1962.

Smith, Robert B. "Rebellion and Repression and the Vietnam War." In James F. Short, Jr., and Marvin E. Wolfgang, (eds.), *Collective Violence.* Chicago: Aldine-Atherton, Inc., 1972, pp. 224-35.

Smith, Thomas S. "Structural Crystallization, Status Inconsistency and Political Partisanship," *American Sociological Review,* Volume 34 (December 1969), pp. 907-21.

Sokol, Robert. "Power Orientation and McCarthyism," *American Journal of Sociology,* Volume 73 (January 1968), pp. 443-52.

Sorel, Georges. *Reflections on Violence.* Translated by T.E. Hulme and J. Roth. New York: The Free Press, 1950.

Spiegel, John P. "The Social and Psychological Dynamics of Militant Negro Activism: A Preliminary Report." Paper delivered at the Winter, 1967 Meetings of the American Academy of Psychoanalysis.

_____. "Violence and the Social Order," *Zygon,* Volume 4 (September 1969), pp. 222-37.

Spilerman, Seymour. "The Causes of Racial Disturbance: A Comparison of Alternative Explanations," *American Sociological Review,* Volume 35 (August 1970), pp. 627-49.

_____. "The Causes of Racial Disturbances: Tests of an Explanation," *American Sociological Review,* Volume 36 (June 1971), pp. 427-42.

_____. "Comments on Wanderer's Article on Riot Severity and its Correlates," *American Journal of Sociology,* Volume 75 (January 1970), pp. 556-60.

Stark, Rodney, and McEvoy, James, III. "Middle Class Violence," *Psychology Today,* (November 1970), pp. 52-4, 110-2.

Stouffer, Samuel A. *Communism, Conformity, and Civil Liberties: A Cross-Section of the Nation Speaks Its Mind.* New York: John Wiley and Sons, Inc., 1955.

Supplemental Studies for the National Advisory Commission on Civil Disorders. Washington, D.C.: U.S. Government Printing Office, 1968.

Templeton, Frederic. "Alienation and Political Participation: Some Research

Findings," *Public Opinion Quarterly,* Volume 30 (Summer 1966), pp. 249-61.

Thompson, Wayne E. and Horton, John E. "Political Alienation as a Force in Political Action," *Social Forces,* Volume 38 (March 1960), pp. 190-5.

———. "Powerlessness and Political Negativism: A Study of Defeated Local Referendums," *American Journal of Sociology,* Volume 67 (March 1962), pp. 485-93.

"Time to Remember 'Forgotten America,' " *Time* (8 August 1969), pp. 42-3.

Tomlinson, T.M. "Ideological Foundations for Negro Action: A Comparative Analysis of Militant and Non-Militant Views of the Los Angeles Riot," *Journal of Social Issues,* Volume 26 (Winter 1970), pp. 93-119.

Treiman, Donald J. "Status Discrepancy and Prejudice," *American Journal of Sociology,* Volume 71 (May 1966), pp. 651-64.

Trotsky, Leon. *Terrorism and Communism: A Reply to Karl Kautsky.* Ann Arbor: University of Michigan Press, 1961.

"The Troubled American: A Special Report on the White Majority," *Newsweek,* (6 October 1969), pp. 29-73.

Tucker, Charles Wright, Jr. "On Working Class Identification," *American Sociological Review,* Volume 31 (December 1966), pp. 855-6.

Tucker, Robert C. *The Marxian Revolutionary Idea.* New York: W.W. Norton and Company, Inc., 1969.

———. *Philosophy and Myth in Karl Marx.* Cambridge: Cambridge University Press, 1961.

Turner, Ralph H. "The Public Perception of Protest," *American Sociological Review,* Volume 34 (December 1969), pp. 815-31.

Verba, Sidney; Brody, Richard A.; Parker, Edwin B.; Nie, Norman H.; Polsby, Nelson W.; Ekman, Paul; and Black, Gordon S. "Public Opinion and the War in Vietnam," *American Political Science Review,* Volume 61 (June 1967), pp. 317-33.

Wanderer, Jules. "An Index of Riot Severity and Some Correlates," *American Journal of Sociology,* Volume 74 (March 1969), pp. 500-5.

Weber, Max. "Class, Status, Party." In H.H. Gerth and C. Wright Mills, (eds.), *From Max Weber: Essays in Sociology.* New York: Oxford University Press, 1946, pp. 180-95.

Wellstone, Paul D. *Black Militants in the Ghetto: Why They Believe in Violence.* Doctoral dissertation, Chapel Hill: University of North Carolina, Department of Political Science, 1969.

Wesolowski, Wlodzimierz. "Marx's Theory of Class Domination: An Attempt at Systematization." In Nicholas Lobkowicz, (ed.), *Marx and the Western World.* Notre Dame: University of Notre Dame Press, 1967, pp. 53-97.

Westergaard, J.H. "The Withering Away of Class: A Contemporary Myth." In Perry Anderson and Robin Blackburn, (eds.), *Towards Socialism.* Ithaca:

Cornell University Press, 1965, pp. 77-113.

Westie, Frank R. "The American Dilemma: An Empirical Test," *American Sociological Review,* Volume 30 (August 1965), pp. 527-38.

_____ . "Negro-White Status Differentials and Social Distance," *American Sociological Review,* Volume 17 (October 1952), pp. 550-8.

_____ . "A Technique for the Measurement of Race Attitudes," *American Sociological Review,* Volume 18 (February 1953), pp. 73-8.

_____ , and Howard, David H. "Social Status Differentials and the Race Attitudes of Negroes," *American Sociological Review,* Volume 19 (October 1954), pp. 584-91.

Wiatr, Jerzy J. "Sociology – Marxism – Reality." In Peter L. Berger, (ed.), *Marxism and Sociology: Views from Eastern Europe.* New York: Appleton-Century-Crofts, 1969, pp. 18-36.

Wiley, Norbert. "America's Unique Class Politics: The Interplay of the Labor, Credit and Commodity Markets," *American Sociological Review,* Volume 32 (August 1967), pp. 529-41.

Williams, Robin M., Jr. *Strangers Next Door: Ethnic Relations in American Communities.* Englewood Cliffs, N.J.: Prentice-Hall, Inc., 1964.

Wilson, James Q., and Banfield, Edward C. "Political Ethos Revisited," *American Political Science Review,* Volume 65 (December 1971), pp. 1048-62.

Wood, Robert C. *The Necessary Majority: Middle America and the Urban Crisis.* New York: Columbia University Press, 1972.

Wright, Nathan, Jr. *Ready To Riot.* New York: Holt, Rinehart and Winston, 1968.

Wrong, Dennis H. "How Important Is Social Class? The Debate Among American Sociologists," *Dissent* (Winter 1972), pp. 278-85.

Zeitlin, Irving M. "The Plain Marxism of C. Wright Mills." In George Fischer, (ed.), *The Revival of American Socialism: Selected Papers of the Socialist Scholars Conference.* New York: Oxford University Press, 1971, pp. 227-43.

Zeitlin, Maurice. *Revolutionary Politics and the Cuban Working Class.* New York: Harper and Row, Publishers, 1970.

Bibliography Addendum

Hamilton, Richard F. *Class and Politics in the United States.* New York: John Wiley and Sons, Inc., 1972.

Marx, Gary T. "Two Cheers for the National Riot Commission." In John Szwed, (ed.), *Black America.* New York: Basic Books, 1970, pp. 78-96.

Muller, Edward N. "A Test of a Partial Theory of Potential for Political Violence," *American Political Science Review,* Volume 66 (September 1972), pp. 928-59.

Sennett, Richard, and Cobb, Jonathan. *The Hidden Injuries of Class.* New York: Alfred A. Knopf, Inc., 1972.

Index

About the Author

Daniel J. Friedman is senior research associate at the Organization for Social and Technical Innovation in Newton, Massachusetts. Dr. Friedman received his A.B. in sociology from Oberlin College, and his Ph.D. in political science from the University of North Carolina at Chapel Hill. His interests include American class politics, and American social policy. He is currently studying unemployment, financial woes, and political extremism.